EVERY LOOK SPEAKS

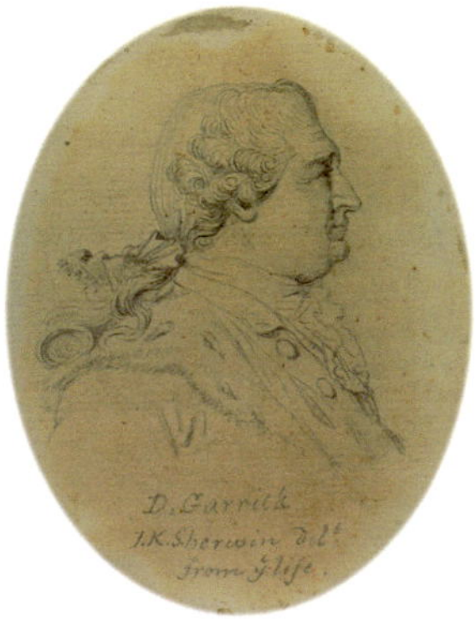

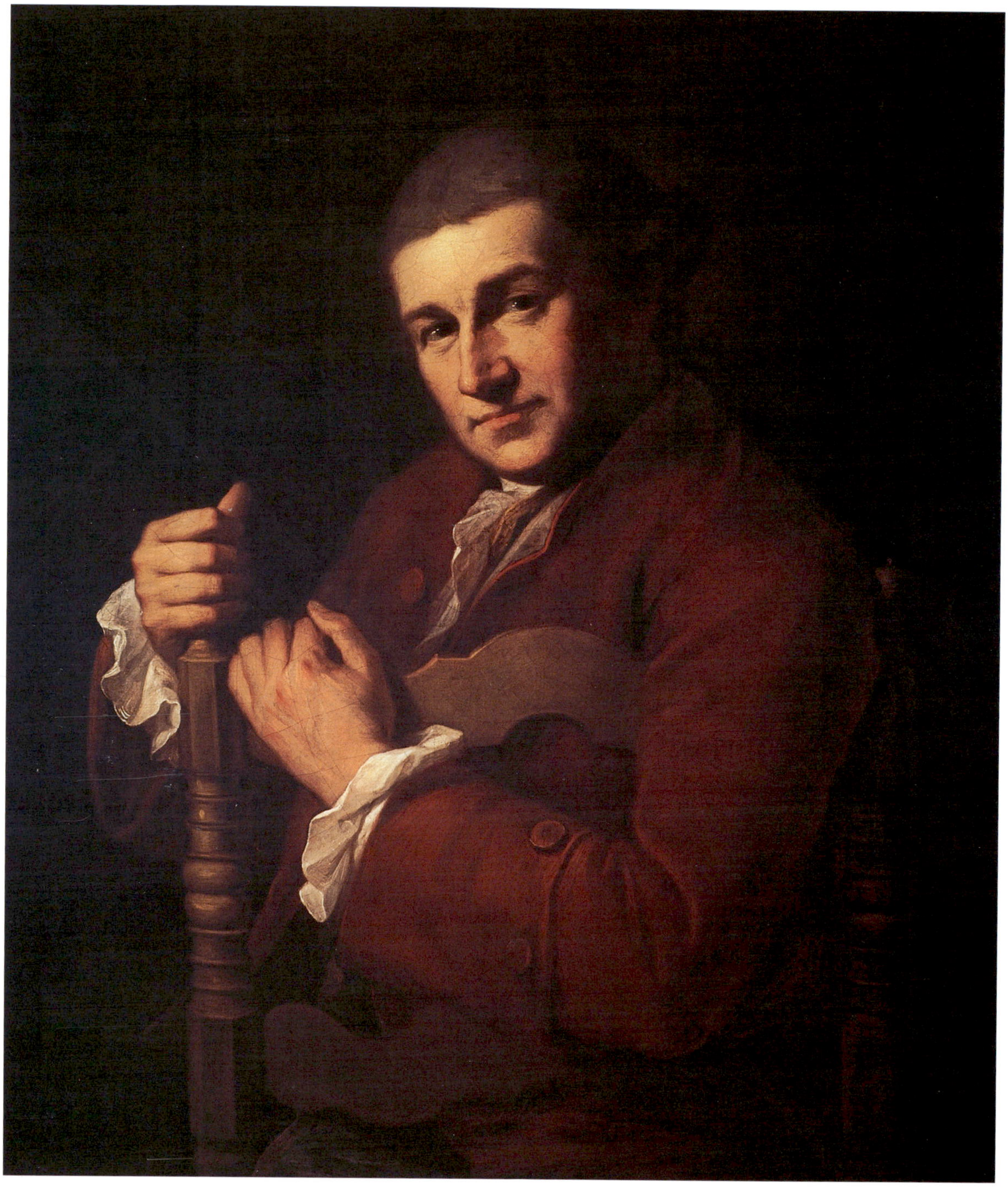

Every Look Speaks

PORTRAITS OF DAVID GARRICK

With an essay by

DESMOND SHAWE-TAYLOR

*

An exhibition at
the Holburne Museum of Art, Bath
16th September to 7th December
2003

*

This catalogue has been published with the support of
The Friends of the Holburne Museum of Art
The Leche Trust
The Paul Mellon Centre for Studies in British Art
MOORE STEPHENS
Chartered Accountants and Independent Financial Advisers, Bath

THE HOLBURNE
MUSEUM OF ART, BATH

GREAT PULTENEY STREET
BATH BA2 4DB

British Library Cataloguing in Publication Data.
A catalogue record for this book is available from the British Library.

ISBN 0 903679 07 8

Design, setting, layout, reprographics printing and binding by Butler & Tanner Limited Frome and London.

Cover illustration Johan Zoffany, David Garrick, cat.no. 23.
The Art Archive / Garrick Club.

Back cover Johan Zoffany, Mr and Mrs Garrick by the Shakespeare Temple, cat no.16.
The Lambton Trustees.

Half title page John Keyse Sherwin, David Garrick, cat. no. 41.
By courtesy of the National Portrait Gallery, London.

Frontispiece Angelica Kauffman, David Garrick, cat. no. 26.
The Burghley House Collection.

CONTENTS

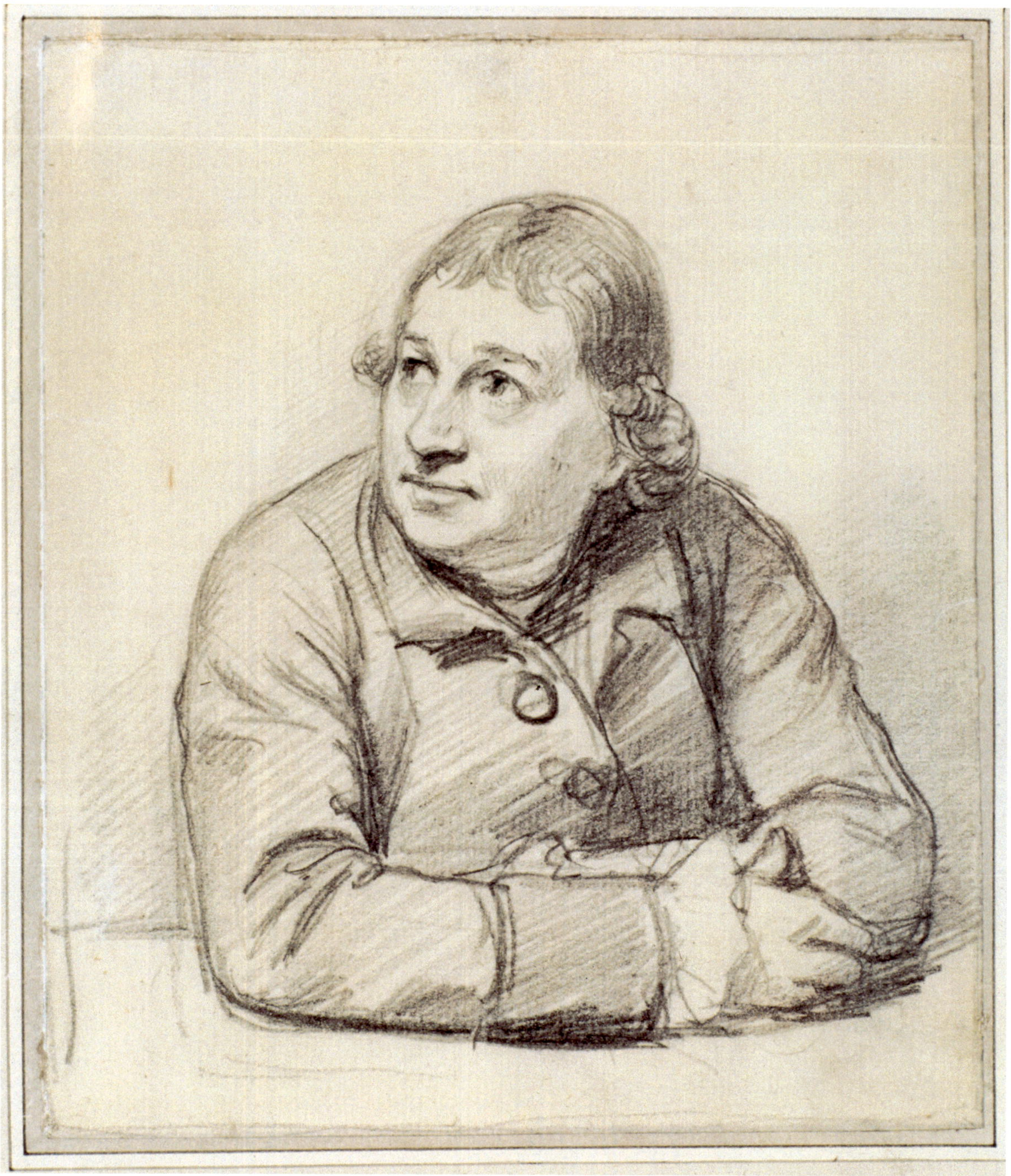

Cat. 39 **Nathaniel Dance,** ***David Garrick*****,** By courtesy of the National Portrait Gallery, London.

INTRODUCTION

*

DAVID W. POSNETT
Chairman of the Board of Trustees, Holburne Museum of Art

An exhibition devoted to the great British Actor, David Garrick, would seem more than fitting for a museum that has just been itself part of a theatrical production in which the Holburne became Lord Steyne's house in a film adaptation of William Thackeray's *Vanity Fair*. We saw not only the transformation of our building for this film, but, equally importantly, how amazing Great Pulteney Street looked with carriages and people bustling about. Bath has not seen so many famous actors on its streets since David Garrick's day.

To David Garrick, Bath was a place of leisure and the arts, 'this land of Circe ... where I do this and do that and do nothing'. I hardly need to remind visitors that actors and painters are both central to Georgian Bath's role as a city of culture as well as pleasure – as our most recent exhibitions have shown – and I believe that this exhibition will be another milestone in the history of the Holburne.

For nearly forty years I have known and loved this period of British Art and the works of the great British painters Gainsborough, Reynolds, and of course Zoffany. The relationship – and hence the interpretation of character – between actors and painters will shine out of this exhibition. Even today no great actor would expect to be painted by so many artists and it is surely only in great painting that the interaction between sitter and painter can be so fully understood.

To use a theatrical analogy, this exhibition has been a major production. It gives me great pleasure to thank Dr. Desmond Shawe-Taylor, Director of the Dulwich Picture Gallery and leading authority on Georgian portraits, for acting as Guest Curator. In-house research has been carried out by Rosie Broadley, who has dedicated many months to unravelling the complexities of Garrick portraiture and iconography. Amina Wright, our Curator of Fine Art, has been responsible for editing the catalogue and for the total organisation. She must have had great pleasure and now satisfaction from obtaining such important loans.

Such an exhibition needs considerable research and for their help I would also like to thank John Ingamells who very kindly let us have a copy of an early draft of his forthcoming catalogue of Later Georgian Portraits in the National Portrait Gallery. The research by Ian McIntyre for his biography of Garrick has been invaluable, and he has also provided a most appropriate and incisive foreword for this catalogue. Ian McIntyre's *Garrick*, published by Allen Lane, was awarded the Theatre Book Prize for 1999. His latest biography, *Joshua Reynolds*, is a second insight into the London literary and artistic circle of the later eighteenth century, and one that will be of great value in the Holburne's future research.

The catalogue has also benefited from contributions by Colin Harrison of the Ashmolean Museum, Dr Susan Sloman, Lisa White our own Curator of Decorative Arts and, above all, Christopher Woodward, the Holburne's energetic Director.

We are also grateful for help with research from Ros Westwood at the Buxton Museum and Art Gallery (who researched lenders to Buxton's Garrick exhibition in 1981), Dr Susan Sloman for her advice on Katherine Read and Gainsborough and his Bath contemporaries, Trevor Fawcett, Catherine Parry-Wingfield, Andrew Kirk and Jim Fowler at the Theatre Museum, Dr Mark Ledbury at the University of Manchester, Charles Noble at Chatsworth and, as ever, Alastair Laing of the National Trust, a member of our Board of Trustees.

As with many other exhibitions here at the Holburne, none

would be possible without ReSource and the Government Indemnity Scheme, and in this connection may I thank them on behalf of the Trustees. Thanks also to all the administrative staff and attendants at the Holburne for taking on the extra work that an exhibition of this size inevitably demands of them.

Sponsorship of this exhibition, for which I express the warm thanks of the Trustees, has come from Moore Stephens (Chartered Accountants and Independent Financial Advisers). Butler & Tanner of Frome have continued to support the design and printing of the Holburne's publications. A grant from the Leche Trust has enabled us to bring Desmond Shawe-Taylor's expertise to the Holburne, and the Paul Mellon Centre for Studies in British Art has covered the cost of illustrating the catalogue. As ever, a special debt of gratitude is due to the Friends of the Holburne Museum for their generous help with the catalogue expenses. Rosie Broadley's time has been greatly assisted by a grant from The Oppenheim Foundation, to whom I express our considerable thanks. Thanks also to Mr & Mrs M.A. Hopkins-Clarke for making it possible for us to illustrate three different views of cat. no. 59.

Finally, I would like to express the Trustees' sincere thanks to all those lenders, named and anonymous, who have so generously lent works from public and private collections.

There were only two paintings which we could not borrow. Hogarth's marriage portrait is on display in the Royal Collection's inaugural exhibition at the Queen's Gallery until the spring of next year, while his *Richard III* cannot leave the Walker Art Gallery because of its fragility; Hogarth painted the actor's face on a separate piece of canvas.

LENDERS

David Alexander
Ashmolean Museum, Oxford
Bristol City Museum and Art Gallery
British Museum
Burghley House Collection
Charlecote Park, The National Trust
Exeter City Museums and Art Gallery
Trustees of the late Sir Brinsley Ford
Garrick Club
Samuel Johnson Birthplace Museum
Lambton Trustees
Lennox-Boyd Collection
Museum of London
National Portrait Gallery
National Museums, Liverpool
Petworth Collection
Her Majesty the Queen
Rothschild Family Trust
Royal Cornwall Museum
Royal Shakespeare Company Collection, Stratford upon Avon
Sir John Soane's Museum
Tate
Theatre Museum
University of Bristol Theatre Collection
Victoria & Albert Museum
Wolverhampton Art Gallery

FOREWORD

*

Ian McIntyre

He had a big nose. He sometimes sought to disguise his lack of inches by building up his shoes with cork heels. As he sat for one of his many portraits, the mischievously mobile play of his features drove his friend Gainsborough to fling down his brush in exasperation.

David Garrick rocketed to instant celebrity as Richard III at the age of 24, and for thirty years, with seemingly effortless versatility he dominated the London stage: 'Damn him!' one of his leading ladies famously exclaimed, 'he could act a gridiron!' He was not only Fondlewife, the jealous old Puritan banker in Congreve's *The Old Bachelor*, but also Bayes, the conceited author in Buckingham's *The Rehearsal*. Joshua Reynolds was so powerfully affected by his farewell appearance as Lear that 'it was full three days before he got the better of it.'

Garrick's fame would spread through France, Germany and Italy – even to Russia, then on the fringe of the civilized world. Yet his importance in the history of the English stage does not derive solely from his reputation as the foremost actor of the eighteenth century. He was also an outstandingly successful manager. 'The theatre engrossed the minds of men to such a degree,' wrote one of his early biographers, 'that there existed in England a *fourth estate*, King, Lords, and Commons, and *Drury-Lane play-house*.'

Then as now, however, celebrity did not always engender universal adulation. Praise there was in plenty, but throughout his career, Garrick found himself at the receiving end of a good deal of blame and abuse, much of it anonymous. His vanity made him a larger target than he might otherwise have presented, but he also excited a good deal of professional jealousy; sometimes, when he arrived to stay at the house of one of his grand friends, he would find waiting for him a grubby letter addressed to 'David Garrick, Player.'

When he retired, he presented his theatrical sword to his old friend Tom King – 'Accept a Small token of our long & constant attachment to Each other' – but very few of his close friends were fellow-actors, and with many of his leading ladies, most notably Mrs Abington, his relations were frequently tempestuous.

He had to wait for the best part of a decade before he was admitted to the Club: 'He will disturb us by his buffoonery,' growled his old mentor and fellow-townsman Johnson. It is more than likely that the great Cham knew very well that one of his former pupil's party turns took the form of grotesque impersonations of himself and his wife Tetty, spied through the keyhole of their bedroom.

Those who loved and admired Garrick did so without reserve. 'Surely he is above Mortality,' Hannah More wrote to her sister after seeing him on stage for the first time. 'His Talents are capacious beyond human credibility. I felt myself annihilated before Him, & every Faculty of my Soul was swallowed up in Attention.'

The lawyer Charles Pratt, raised to the peerage as Lord Camden in 1765 and appointed Lord Chancellor the following year, was another close friend. Agreeably indolent, fond of music and the theatre, he was a stylish and charming letter-writer. 'Dear Garrick,' he wrote on one occasion: 'It is such a long time since we met, that I begin to feel that kind of desire to see you and Mrs Garrick that makes a Swiss sick when he has been absent any considerable time from his own country.'

For a quarter of a century or more, Garrick and Joshua Reynolds saw a great deal of each other socially. Only in the 1940s, with the discovery of the Boswell papers at Malahide Castle, did it emerge that the painter's admiration for the actor did not extend to the man. 'Garrick,' Reynolds wrote, 'had no friends to whom he gave orders that he was always at home, except to his doctors, of which he had two sorts, one sort administering for his body, the other for his diseased mind – in other words, his vanity.' And then, this savage envoi: 'The first were generally quacks and the others sycophants.'

He did not absent himself from Garrick's funeral, for all that. There were thirty-six mourning coaches, each drawn by six horses, and Reynolds took his place with Charles James Fox in one of five allotted to members of the Club. The arrangements had been in the hands of Sheridan, and there were those who thought he had gone some way over the top. 'The Court,' Horace Walpole wrote with feline glee, 'was delighted to see a more noble and splendid appearance at the interment of a comedian than had waited on the remains of the great Earl of Chatham.'

The best known of the tributes that appeared in the months following Garrick's death was that written by Sheridan and spoken at Drury Lane by Mrs Yates. He passed in review the 'pure and liquid tone' of Garrick's speech, his mastery of gesture and silence, his grace of action. And he contrasted the ephemeral nature of the actor's art with the enduring achievement of the poet, the sculptor or the painter:

> The actor, only, shrinks from Time's award;
> Feeble tradition is his memory's guard;
> By whose faint breath his merits must abide,
> Unvouch'd by proof — to substance unallied!

The son of a French father, Garrick was to discover during the two visits he paid to France that he was in some ways taken more seriously there than at home – rather as Peter Brook would be two centuries later. The *beau monde* and the literati he met in Paris saw acting not just as a form of entertainment but as one of the fine arts, and his name and reputation there were to prove remarkably enduring. Diderot, for example, would invite his comments on his essay *Le Paradoxe sur le Comédien* before it was published, and in revolutionary France, when critics wrote about the celebrated tragedian François-Joseph Talma, it was Garrick with whom he was most frequently compared.

When Frank Hedgcock was preparing a thesis on Garrick for presentation to the Sorbonne in the early years of the last century, he was told a curious tale by a French academic. As a child, his mother used to warn him that if he was not good, 'Garrigues the Englishman' would come and get him – 'the threat was accompanied with a grimace that perpetuated the actor's reputation as a pantomimist.'

An ogre. A bogeyman. Not merely famous, but the stuff of legend in the land of his forebears. That would have tickled Garrick's vanity most deliciously.

As would the knowledge that more than two hundred years after his death, he and that fugitive art of which he was master would be so handsomely celebrated in this exhibition. Sheridan was guilty of poetic licence. 'Feeble tradition' is not, after all, his memory's sole guard.

'THE BEAUTIFUL STROKES OF A GREAT ACTOR'

Garrick and his painters

*

DESMOND SHAWE-TAYLOR

Oh what a pity it is that the strong and beautiful strokes of a great actor should not be as lasting as the strokes of the pencil or the chisel of inferior artists.

COLLEY CIBBER, 1740[1]

David Garrick (1716–1779) was more often painted in his lifetime than anyone in England, with the exception of the reigning monarch. This essay asks why Garrick wanted to have himself painted so often, why artists were so happy to oblige, and to what extent Garrick helped them to create the resulting paintings.

Garrick *could* have himself painted often because he was rich. He prospered as actor and as manager of Drury Lane Theatre from 1747 until his retirement in 1776. He married in 1749 a successful dancer, Eva Maria Violette (1725–1822), who enjoyed the patronage of the Earl and Countess of Burlington, and the couple lived like 'the quality' at the country house Garrick bought himself next to the Thames at Hampton in 1754. From time to time people might snipe at this jumped-up player, as when Horace Walpole warns his friend, Sir Horace Mann, the British Envoy in Florence, 'be a little on your guard, remember he is *an actor*!'[2] There is little other evidence that Mr and Mrs Garrick did not move effortlessly in intellectual circles and high society, just as well as the aristocratic Horace Walpole. When Garrick took up collecting old masters while on the Grand Tour of Italy he wrote to Lord Burlington: 'I don't see why I should not be a little ridiculous, as well as My betters'.[3] Exactly the same could be said of sitting for a portrait. There are many portraits of Mr and Mrs Garrick by artists who specialised in depicting the English aristocracy. In Paris in 1751 they visited the studio of the fashionable Swiss portrait painter, Jean-Etienne Liotard (1702–1789), for a pair of pastels, which they gave to the Earl and Countess of Burlington.[4] While in Rome on his Grand Tour of 1764, Garrick sat for the most sought-after portrait painter of the century, Pompeo Batoni (1708–1787, cat. no. 25). This is of course not an ordinary *Milordi* portrait: the 1736 edition of Terence's *Comedies*, which Garrick points to in the portrait, might be typical of the kind of antiquarian interest Batoni likes to celebrate in his English sitters, but here there is the special twist that the page is open on a series of drawings of ancient theatrical masks.[5] These act as symbolic attributes of Comedy and Tragedy, like those in Zoffany's portrait of a year earlier (cat. no. 21); they also remind us that Garrick could adopt any of these expressions at will.

The most interesting 'straight' portrait is that by Reynolds, exhibited at the Royal Academy in 1773 as a 'Gentleman and Lady' (cat. no. 42).[6] It is surely surprising how unlike professional performers this couple seem. Garrick has broken off reading; his wife muses upon what she has heard. The abstracted expressions and parkland setting are common devices at this date, used to celebrate tender feelings and marital love.[7] We are here deliberately intended to forget that 'he is *an actor*!'

It is striking how many of the portraits featured in this exhibition were given as presents. For Samuel Johnson

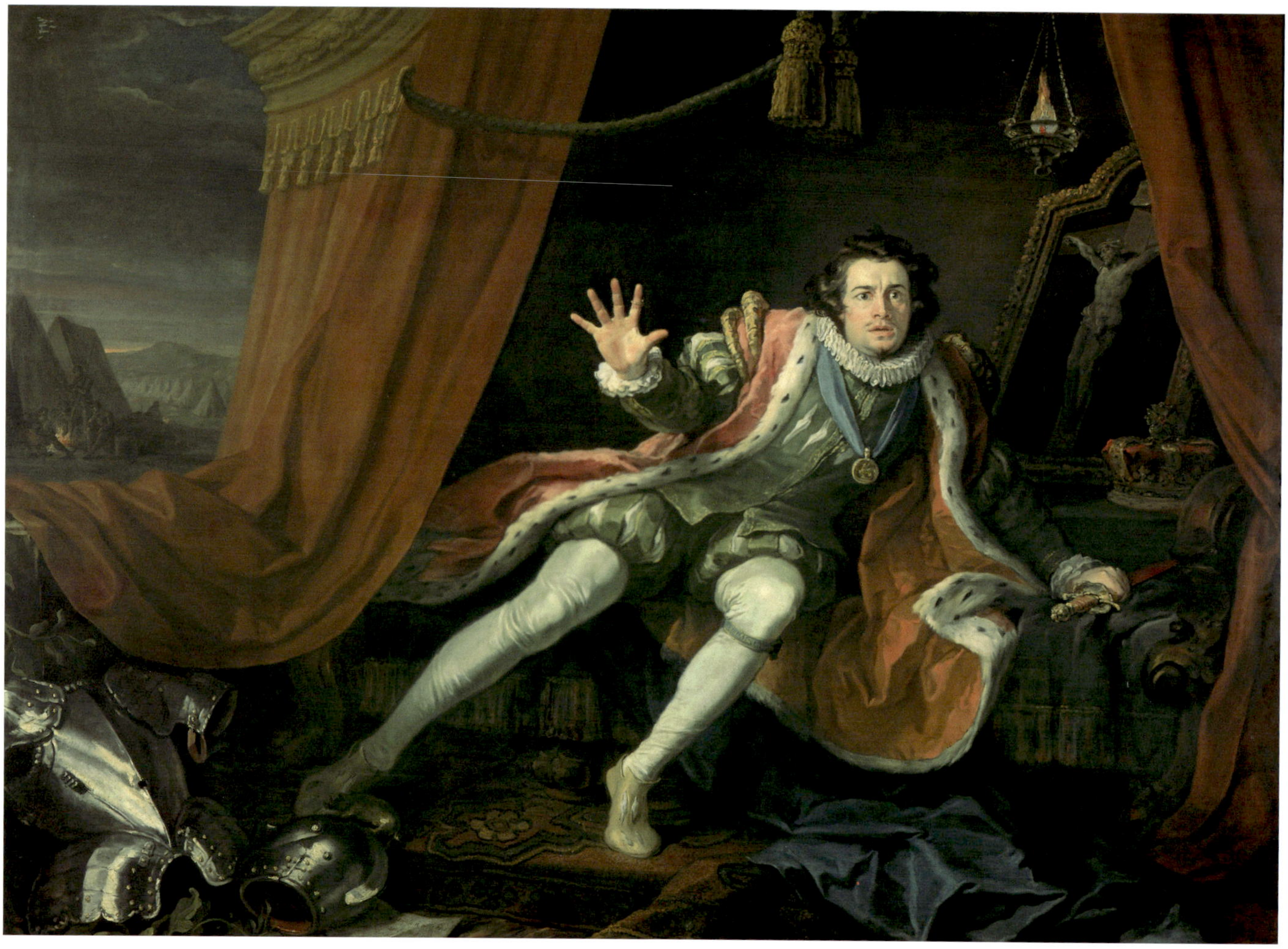

FIG. 1 William Hogarth (1697–1764), *David Garrick as Richard III, 1746* oil on canvas, 190.5 × 251.2 cm, National Museums Liverpool (The Walker).

(1709–1784), the value of portraiture lay 'in diffusing friendship, in reviving tenderness, in quickening the affection of the absent, and continuing the presence of the dead.'[8] The idea of portraits as tokens of friendship is centuries old: in 1517 two friends, Desiderius Erasmus and Petrus Aegidius, had themselves painted by Quinten Massys, the two portraits were hinged together like a diptych and sent to another friend, Sir Thomas More.[9] Garrick did something similar when in 1763 he planned to exchange portraits with his tricky rival James Quin (1693–1766) as 'Tokens of good Will between us'; or when in 1774 he swapped his portrait for a landscape painted by his friend, John Taylor of Bath.[10] This diffusion of friendship sometimes affects the appearance as well as the eventual home of a portrait. In 1745 Francis Hayman painted a double portrait of David Garrick and William Windham, probably in Bath, but with a landscape background suggesting Windham's country house, Felbrigg Hall (fig. 2). In the same year Garrick wrote to Hayman, with a characteristic example of Georgian 'male bonding': 'damn all formality between Us.'[11] This portrait celebrates the informality of friendship; the way in which William Windham gestures to the viewer includes the third friend, the artist, in the circle. There is a similar friendly complicity between sitter and viewer (and therefore between sitter and painter friend) in Hogarth's double portrait of 1757 (fig. 4). Gainsborough's 1772 portrait of Garrick (cat. no. 38) seems even more engaging and affectionate when we learn that Gainsborough planned to copy the picture 'to hang in my own Parlour, not as a show Picture, but for my own enjoyment'.[12]

Clubbable informality is not the only mood which can be

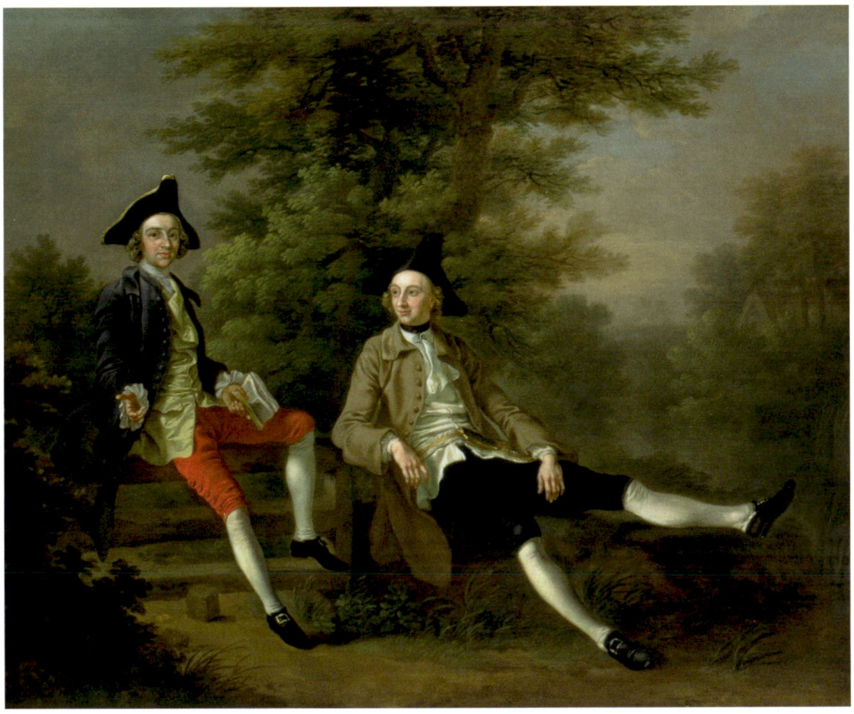

FIG. 2 Francis Hayman (1708–1776)
David Garrick and William Windham of Felbrigg, *c. 1745*
oil on canvas, 85 × 102 cm
Private Collection, Bridgeman Art Library.

expressed in 'friendship portraits': Zoffany's image of Garrick painted for his friend and collaborator George Colman the Elder in 1763 (cat. no. 21) expresses the esteem in which the actor was held. It follows the format of a coin or medal, which was a standard way of conveying veneration: Garrick is shown paying contemplative homage to a medallion of Shakespeare in Van der Gucht's portrait (cat. no. 35)[13]. In 1725 Jonathan Richardson recommended that 'Painters should take a Face and make an Antique Medal, or Bas-Relief of it, by divesting it of its Modern Disguises, raising the Air, and the Features, and giving the Dress of those Times, and suitable to the Character intended.'[14] The first 'modern disguise' which Garrick has 'divested himself of' is his wig; the resulting emphasis of the egg-shape of the head follows exactly the low relief conventions of a coin; if it doesn't exactly look Classical at least it looks timeless, as does Garrick's open shirt and grave, aspiring expression. The most likely direct source for the painting and its allegorical stone frame, making it into a sort of monument to Garrick's art, is Kneller's 1721 portrait of Alexander Pope (fig. 3).[15]

Garrick also considered self-promotion when he had his portrait painted. He wrote from Paris on 20 November 1764 to his brother George:

I am so plagu'd here for my Prints or rather Prints of me – that I must desire You to send me by ye first opportunity *six* prints from Reynolds's picture, you may apply to the graver he lives in Leicester Fields, and his name is Fisher, he will give you good ones, if he knows they are for me – You must likewise send me a *King Lear* by *Wilson*, *Hamlet* d[itto], *Jaffier* & Belv[ider] by *Zoffani*, speak to him for two or 3, & what Else he may have done of Me – There is likewise a print of Me, as I am, from Liotard's picture Scrap'd by MacArdel, send me 2 or 3 of them, speak to MacArdel, & any other prints of Me, if tolerable, that I can't remember.[16]

Most of these images can be seen in this exhibition (see cat. nos 11 and 12, 13, 18, 19 and 20, and 6). Garrick must have used these prints like the signed photographs which Divas dispense to back-stage admirers. Garrick was probably more concerned with prints, than the paintings from which they were derived. Hogarth's portrait of Garrick as Richard III (fig. 1) was the artist's initiative; but Garrick was certainly keenly interested in the print made after it (cat. no. 4). Examples of paintings in this exhibition, which hung in Garrick's rooms in the Adelphi and at his country house at Hampton, show that he was not above using real paintings to enhance his image.[17]

But of course the main reason for any actor wanting a

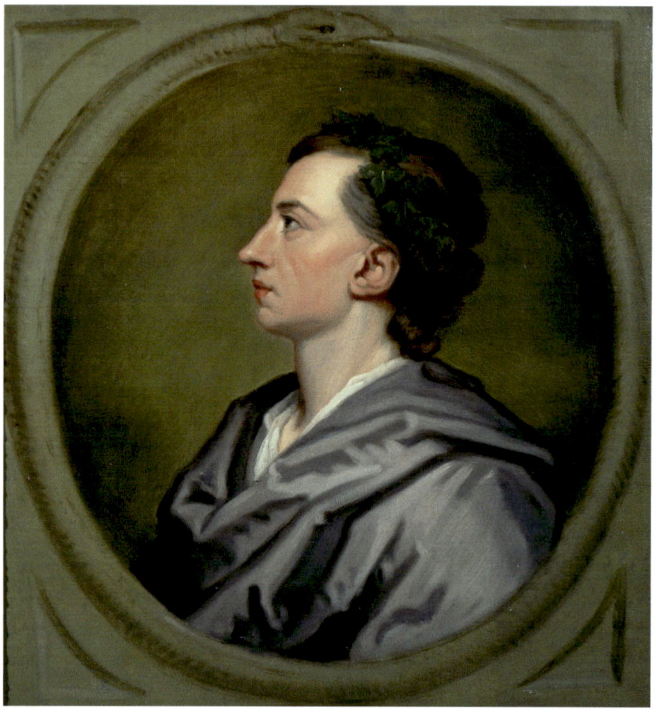

FIG. 3 **Studio of Sir Godfrey Kneller (1646–1729)** *Alexander Pope, c. 1721* **oil on canvas,** Philip Mould, Historical Portraits Ltd, London, Bridgeman Art Library.

portrait of him or herself at work is summed up by the words of Colley Cibber which head this essay: the 'beautiful strokes' of the pencil (as the paint brush was then called) are more durable than those of the actor.

Why should painters want to paint Garrick? Certainly not just because they received commissions from him: at least two important portraits were executed by and for the artist. All eighteenth-century British artists executed portraits, and most complained of the drudgery of it. The problem was that most sitters were so dull there was no character to depict and so obscure that nobody (save the sitter's family) was interested in the result. Portrait painters of the period generally produce their best work for celebrities, whose characters were known (at least in a public way), and whose images could bring fame and (through sales of prints) *some* fortune to an artist. Garrick was an ideal sitter: he was certainly interesting and was famous enough to make the name of any painter, however obscure, or improve the reputation of any painter, however exalted. Hogarth's *Garrick as Richard III* (fig. 1) was probably not undertaken on commission, though it soon found a buyer in William Duncombe of Duncombe Park, Yorkshire. Hogarth makes it quite clear that the record £200 he received for the painting was paid because of the sitter not the subject.[18] Similarly Reynolds seems to have undertaken his *Garrick between Tragedy and Comedy* (cat. no.11) 'at risk', though he sold it to George Montagu-Dunk, 2nd Earl of Halifax, for about 300 guineas, having also made a splash with it at the exhibition of the Society of Artists in 1762.[19] It is difficult to determine the origin of Angelica Kauffmann's portrait of Garrick, executed in Rome during his Tour in 1764 (cat. no. 26), but it is likely, as Rosie Broadley suggests below, that it was undertaken at the artist's instigation and used by her as a 'calling card' on her visit to London.[20] If this is so, it might explain why it is so unlike Kauffmann's normal decorative version of Neo-Classicism. Its dark shadows, flickering touch, effect of down-to-earth reality and arresting, casual pose are all characteristics of Dutch seventeenth-century portraiture. Angelica Kauffmann uses her 'Dutch Brushes' for one other painting – a 1767 portrait of Sir Joshua Reynolds (The National Trust, Saltram).[21] Perhaps this is a manner she used to characterise 'North Sea' sitters and one which she calculated would 'play well' in London. When the Cantonese sculptor, Chitqua, came to London in 1769 wishing to advertise his skills, it was through a speculatively undertaken figure of Garrick that he did so (cat. no. 38).

The other advantage of Garrick was that he posed in a lively and expressive way, though actually this could be infuriating. According to his obituary in 1788, Gainsborough

> never found any portrait so difficult to hit as that of Mr Garrick, for when he was sketching in the eyebrows, and thought he had hit upon their precise situation, and looked a second time at his model, he found the eyebrows lifted up to the middle of his forehead and when he a third time looked they were dropped like a curtain close over the eyes: so flexible and universal was the countenance of this great player.[22]

Hogarth was forced to alter the *Richard III* so many times than in the end he had to stick a fresh piece of canvas over the face and start again.[23] Zoffany achieved his restful image of Garrick (cat. no. 21) only by spying on him from the next-door room.

Is there then an art to posing? Did Garrick create his own images? In which case, how important was he for the story of eighteenth-century British painting? One thing Garrick

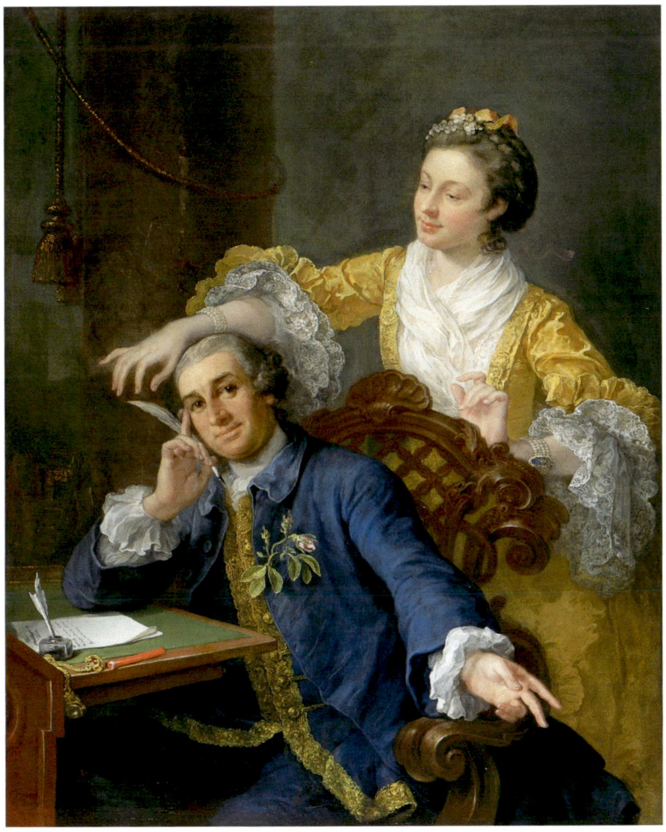

FIG. 4 **William Hogarth (1697–1764),** ***David and Eva Maria Garrick, 1757*** **oil on canvas, 132.6 × 104.2 cm,** The Royal Collection © 2003, Her Majesty Queen Elizabeth II.

did *not* do was to associate himself with a particular style of painting. He sat with equal enthusiasm for Rococo portraits early in his career and Neo-classical portraits late in his career. At his debut in the 1740s painting was dominated by the modern French style, which favoured light tonalities, bright colours, curling – deliberately decorative – outlines and a polite 'gallant' mood. Francis Hayman's *c.*1747 image of Garrick and Mrs Pritchard in Benjamin Hoadly's *The Suspicious Husband* (cat. no. 7), is a perfect example of the type, with its exaggerated gestures and shimmering, silvery surfaces. At the time of Garrick's retirement in 1776, British painting had moved to a style more influenced by the old masters, so that artists tended to use darker shadows, more muted colours, simplified outlines and a more sober or contemplative mood. Reynolds's portrait of Garrick as Kitely (cat. no. 29) and Gainsborough's 1770 portrait of Garrick reading (cat. no. 38) are both examples of the type.

Though Garrick moved happily with the times, his artist friends did not. Hogarth was the only artist of the period who adopted a Rococo style as a point of principle: his *Analysis of Beauty* of 1753 is a brilliant exposition of the delights of its decorative complexity. Unfortunately, the treatise was written just as the style was falling out of fashion. Four years later, in 1757, Hogarth painted a double portrait of Garrick and his wife (fig. 4), which appears to be a defiant Rococo manifesto: the paint is applied with a breadth and a softness which responds to recent developments in painting, but the elaborately scrolling lines of the clothes, the light tone, brilliant colour and gallant mood are all pure Rococo. Even the literally serpentine chair belongs with the polemic: it was designed by Hogarth for Garrick's Shakespeare Temple (seen in cat. no. 16) and made of the wood of Shakespeare's own sacred mulberry tree.[24] Garrick may have appreciated these ideas and certainly continued to value Hogarth's work (see below), yet a few years later he was sitting for Reynolds for a similarly gallant scene (cat. no. 11), but one painted in the new 'old master' style.

Garrick's importance for painters lies in the overlap between the arts of acting and painting, where his 'day job' could really be brought to bear. When an artist paints an actor it is impossible to say exactly who has contributed what; all that we can identify are the elements in the work, which *could have* derived from the actor's art as well as from the painter's art. Thus we gain an insight into the sort of dialogue that might have occurred during the sitting. Before examining the ways in which the theories of the two arts overlapped in the period it is worth giving some idea of Garrick's approach to his own art.

Garrick was a scholarly and articulate actor-manager, who enjoyed collecting manuscripts for old plays and also amassed an impressive general library. He had a particularly fine collection of bound volumes of prints after antiquities and old master paintings; he even had an important group of sixteenth and seventeenth-century Emblem books, of a type normally consulted only by painters. He enjoyed the friendship of writers, politicians and, as we have seen, artists. Garrick was evidently an excellent producer and teacher. The watchmen in the brawl scene from the *Provok'd Wife* (cat. no. 22) of 1763 (and many other theatrical paintings from the period) provide us with a direct insight into the remarkable quality of ensemble acting at Drury Lane under Garrick's management. Kitty Clive (see cat. no. 63) wrote on 23 January 1776:

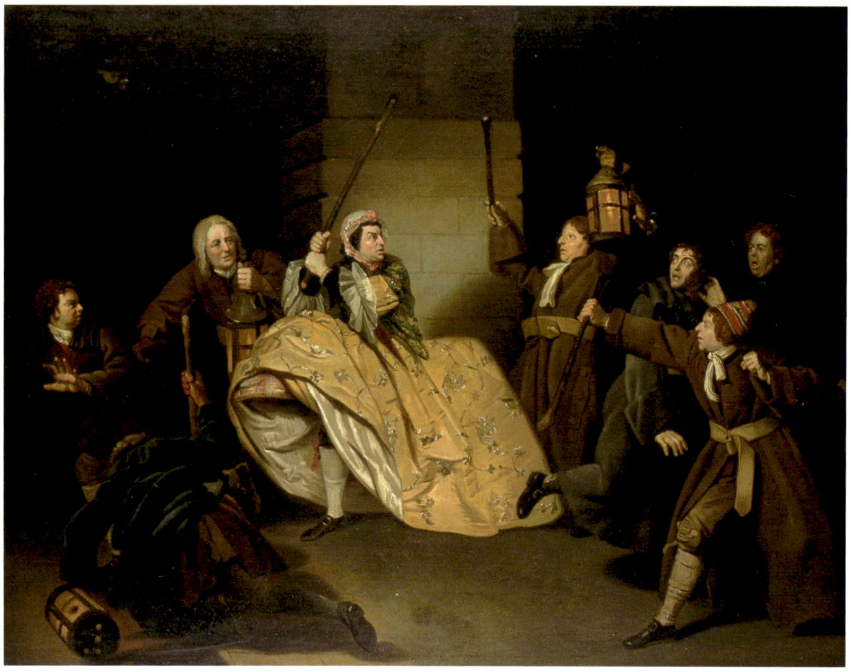

CAT. 22 Johan Zoffany
David Garrick in 'The Provok'd Wife'
Wolverhampton Art Gallery.

> I have seen you, with your magical hammer in your hand, *endeavouring* to beat your ideas into the heads of creatures who had none of their own – I have seen you, with lamb-like patience, endeavouring to make them comprehend you; and I have seen you when that could not be done – I have seen your lamb turned into a lion: by this your great labour and pains the public was entertained; *they* thought they all acted very fine, – they did not see you pull the wires.[25]

Perhaps it could be said of the artists in this exhibition, '*they* thought they all painted very fine, – they did not see David Garrick pull the wires.'

So what could actors and artists talk about? Since the Renaissance, artists were advised to befriend writers in order that they could help them in the understanding and interpretation of the texts, which they sought to render in paint. Garrick was a writer as well as actor and advised his friend Francis Hayman at considerable length over his illustrations to Sir Thomas Hanmer's edition of Shakespeare's plays. In 1745 he writes suggesting that the climax of Othello is not the *action* of suffocating Desdemona but the *revelation* of Iago's treachery.[26] The vivid word-picture of a scene from Lear is quoted below (cat. no. 7): Garrick advises Hayman to show the King *seated*, again in such a way as to suggest his complex and pitiful state of mind, rather than his heroic railing at the storm.[27] Incidentally, it is interesting that when Garrick is shown in the part (cat. no. 13), the expressions are very similar to those described in the letter, but his Lear *stands*, breasting the storm, rather than lying on the ground, which would have seemed at that date a very abject and unkinglike posture. In his letter Garrick goes on to assure Hayman 'I shall better make you conceive My Notion of this Attitude & Expression when I see you.'

What sort of things might go into these 'attitudes and expressions' that Garrick is so eager to discuss? This is the overlap between the two arts and can best be explained by a summary of the literature on the subject, which it is safe to assume Garrick would have known about through conversations with friends like Dr Johnson, and in many cases would actually have read. The earliest discussion of how actors and artists might express emotions or ideas without words comes in ancient treatises on the subject of Oratory – the lawyer or the statesman's art of persuasion. Quintilian in his *Institutio Oratoria* of *c.* 96 AD describes the postures appropriate to various types of passage in a speech – denunciation, eulogy or whatever – in a way that directly influenced English treatises on the Theatre. By the eighteenth century material of this kind was available in

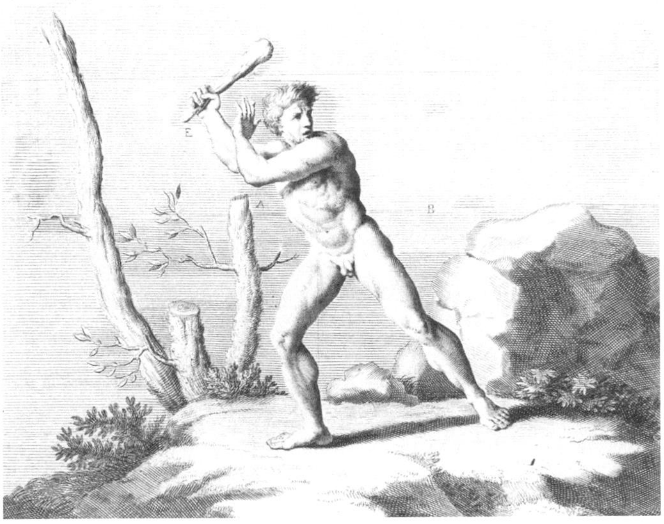

FIG. 5 From Leonardo da Vinci's *Trattato della Pittura*, Paris 1651, (illustration based on a drawing by Nicholas Poussin 1594–1665) Cambridge University Library.

illustrated guides for ease of use. Posture in action was discussed in Leonardo's *Treatise on Painting*, which existed in manuscript form and was first published in Paris in 1651 with illustrations based on drawings by Nicolas Poussin (fig. 5). The similarity between these plates and depictions of Garrick in action – as Jaffier in *Venice Preserv'd* (See cat. no. 40); as Richard III, painted by Nathaniel Dance (cat. no. 40); as Sir John Brute in *The Provok'd Wife* (cat. no. 22) – suggest that he and his painters knew the work.

The discussion of expression in the period was completely dominated by a lecture given in 1698 at the French Academy, by its first president, Charles Le Brun, called *Conférence sur L'Expression*. Le Brun provided diagrammatic illustrations for his treatise (fig. 6) which was published under various titles in French, English and many other languages throughout the eighteenth century and provided an easy crib for those wishing to represent 'Veneration', 'Scorn', 'Horror', 'Hope' etc. Garrick 'did' Le Brun expressions as a party piece![28] One account tells us that at a dinner in Paris in 1763:

> the conversation turned upon the delineation of the passions, in the course of which Mr. Garrick made many judicious observations, and illustrated them by alternately throwing his features into the representation of Love, Hatred, Terror, Pity, Jealousy, Desire, Joy in so rapid and striking a manner as astounded the whole company who acknowledged it was the finest instance of *'nature'* that they had ever met with.[29]

It is fascinating that something, which sounds to us so artificial, was hailed as a triumph of Nature; but we should remember that Le Brun's diagrams were regarded as scientific analysis, rather than artistic convention. The huge impact of Le Brun's work can be seen by comparing one of his diagrams (fig. 6) with Garrick's expression as Richard III in Hogarth's painting (fig. 1); as Hamlet in Wilson's painting (cat. no. 8) and as Macbeth in Zoffany's painting (cat. no. 30).

Expression showed what you felt; *physiognomy* showed what you were. This science attempted to show how temperament could be read from a person's face *and* body. A treatise on the subject by Aristotle survives from antiquity and was brought up to date in 1598 by an Italian, Giovanni Battista della Porta, in his *Della Fisonomia dell'Huomo*. Both Reynolds and Garrick would have been aware from this tradition of writing that Ben Jonson's Kitely (cat. no. 29) was feeling jealous but was also of a jealous *temperament* or 'complexion'. It is this that may explain the bloodless, jaundiced complexion in Reynolds's painting. Incidentally

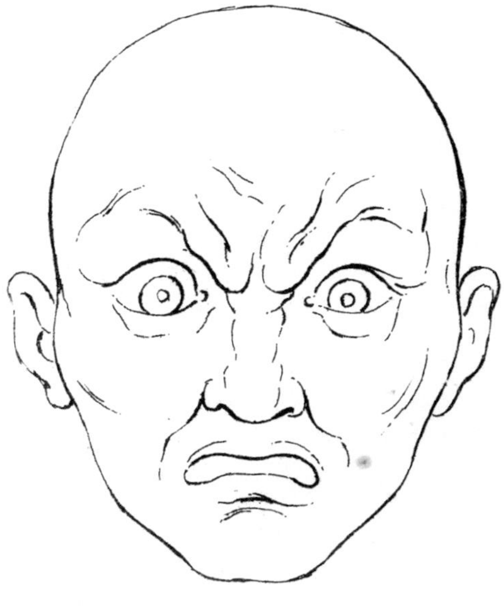

FIG 6. Charles Le Brun (1619–1690), 'Horror' from *Méthode pour apprendre à dessiner les Passions*, edition of 1702, Cambridge University Library.

the fact that 'complexion' means both skin colour and character – as in 'his complexion is perfect gallows' (*The Tempest*, Act I, scene 1) – is an indication of how deeply the concepts of the science of physiognomy are ingrained in the language.

Posture wasn't just expressive, it was also polite. Manuals like Nivelon's *Rudiments of Genteel Behaviour* of 1737 taught you how to stand, bow, exchange gifts and take tea like a gentleman (or lady). Garrick was greatly admired for the grace of his posture, an accomplishment that was regarded as especially difficult to attain for those who were not gentlemen by birth. A year after his London debut (in 1742) readers of *The Gentleman's Magazine* were assured, 'Mr. Garrick is of middling stature, yet being well proportioned and having a peculiar happiness in his address and action is a living instance that it is not essential to a theatrical hero to be six foot high'.[30] This is the point of Hogarth's comic drawing of 1746 demonstrating that *proportionally* little Davy is in fact taller than his giant rival, James Quin (cat. no. 5). According to his early biographer, Thomas Davies, his Grand Tour in 1764–5 made his deportment even more graceful and his manner more elegant.[31] Fine posture was essential for tragedy, where the heroes are always noble, and a great advantage in comedy. The German writer Georg Christian Lichtenberg describes Garrick as Archer in *The Beaux' Stratagem*, when he plays a gentleman disguised as a servant. Archer falls into conversation with a real servant, Scrub, who is dazzled by his silk stockings and stylish way of slinging one foot across the other knee.[32] The entire humour of the scene depended upon Scrub's furtive and pitiful attempts to imitate this most inimitable accomplishment. Garrick could also do bad posture: there are no manuals called the *Rudiments of Plebeian Behaviour* but, if there were, his Abel Drugger (cat. no. 36 and fig. 9) would provide the perfect illustration, as can be seen by comparing his posture with the stylish con men behind him. It is the parallel feet that really give him away. Garrick himself wrote about this role in his anonymous essay on acting:

> His toes must be *inverted* from the Heel, and by *holding* his *Breath*, he will unavoidably give himself a *Tremor* in the *Knees*, and if his *Fingers*, at the same Time, seem *Convuls'd*, it finishes the compleatest low Picture of *Grotesque Terror* that can be imagin'd by a *Dutch* painter.[33]

This passage is a useful way of bringing us up short and at the same time taking stock of the learning outlined above. Clearly Garrick can 'take apart' a character and enumerate its component elements of posture, action and expression; yet what struck contemporaries about his depiction of Abel Drugger was that he didn't seem to be *doing* anything, except standing around looking gormless. The comedy lay in this natural understated style. Lichtenberg describes in detail the way in which Garrick's Drugger believes himself master of the situation depicted here, rather than its victim:

> the effect of this judicious restraint is indescribable, for one did not see him as a simpleton being gulled, but as a much more ridiculous creature, with an air of secret triumph, thinking himself the slyest of rogues.[34]

Such a subtle theatrical double bluff doesn't seem like acting, it seems as if Garrick is, in the words of another member of the audience, presenting the 'Face of Inanity'.[35] A grocer from Garrick's home town of Lichfield saw a performance and returned home bitterly disappointed, telling Garrick's brother Peter, 'Tho' he is your brother, Mr. Garrick, he is one of the shabbiest, meanest, most pitiful hounds I ever saw in the whole course of my life'.[36] More sophisticated theatre-goers realised that Abel Drugger was a marker Garrick had set down at one end of his repertoire: Joseph Warton in 1756 congratulated Great Britain on

> two very singular phenomena; I mean, Shakespeare's being able to portray characters so very different as FALSTAFF, and MACBETH; and Garrick's being able to personate so inimitably LEAR, or an ABLE DRUGGER. Nothing can more fully demonstrate the extent and versatility of these two original geniuses.[37]

You can't make yourself look this insignificant by reading Quintilian.

We have seen the kind of intellectual framework shared by actors and artists, but to examine how these collaborations might work in practice it is worth taking four case-studies of important artists whom Garrick especially inspired – Hogarth, Zoffany, Reynolds and Gainsborough. Hogarth was twenty years older than Garrick and cut his teeth as an artist depicting a previous generation of actor. But it was almost certainly he who asked Garrick to sit for him as Richard III in 1745 (fig. 1), rather than the other way around. The work is of great significance for Hogarth. In the previous decade he had painted some history paintings (as opposed to 'modern moral subjects', as he called them); Garrick himself bought his *Falstaff Examining Recruits* (Private Collection) and *Satan, Sin and Death* (cat. no. 53), as well as the more typically Hogarthian *Election* Series (Sir John Soane's Museum).[38] Hogarth's most ambitious Shakespearean subject was the bizarre *Scene from the Tempest* of *c.* 1735 (National Trust, Nostell Priory), which is really a small-scale and 'highly seasoned' version of an Adoration of the Shepherds. Altogether there was little to justify the inclusion of a copy of Shakespeare in his *Self-Portrait* of 1745 (Tate), the same year as *Garrick as Richard III.* The fact was that Hogarth's portrait style had advanced dramatically in the early 1740s, but he had not translated this new style into proper 'subject pictures'. Garrick provided an ideal opportunity. Hogarth paints the figure and the attributes – tent, armour, carpet and curtain – with the robust directness of his portraiture and with a confidence certainly not seen in his previous heroic subject pictures.

Hogarth's previous Shakespearean subjects had all included elements of the grotesque; in some ways Garrick helps him to present a potentially grotesque character with the heroic dignity of a history painting. Descriptions of Garrick in this part constantly stress how much he is the King and how little the hunchback of Shakespeare's text. Arthur Murphy recorded the moment seen in Hogarth's image:

> His soliloquy in the tent scene discovered the inward man ... When he started from his dream he was a spectacle of horror. He called out in a manly voice 'Give me another horse', he paused, and with a countenance of dismay, advanced crying out in a tone of distress, 'Bind up my wounds', and then, falling on his knees, said in a most piteous accent, 'Have mercy heaven!'.[39]

Joseph Warton in his *Essay on the Writings and Genius of Pope* of 1756 makes it quite clear that he regards this painting as unique in Hogarth's career:

> In the serious pieces, into which Hogarth has deviated from the natural bias of his genius, there are some strokes of the Ridiculous discernible, which suit not the dignity of the subject. In his PREACHING OF ST PAUL, a dog snarling at a cat; and in his PHAROAH'S DAUGHTER, the figure of the infant Moses, who expresses archness rather than timidity, are alleged as instanced, that this artist unrivalled in his own walk, could not resist the impulse of his imagination towards drollery. His picture, however, of Richard III is pure and unmix'd with any ridiculous circumstances, and strongly expresses terror and amazement.[40]

This painting uses the arresting device (quite common in the history of art) of the main figure looking out at the viewer, which is here subtly adapted by having Richard look just over our shoulder at a ghost that seems to be creeping up behind us. His expression is one of 'Horror' taken from Le Brun's prescriptions (fig. 6). Garrick sees a ghost, or is caught at the moment of waking from a nightmare while the image of a 'ghost' is still present in his mind. But Hogarth does not depict a ghost. The result is an expressive truncation: we see terror but not the source of that terror. This is the depiction of a state of mind; it is a 'historical moral subject' dealing with a guilty conscience. The version of the play Garrick actually performed (adapted by Colley Cibber) expresses Hogarth's intention better than Shakespeare's original. This passage begins with the final words of the ghost of Henry VI:

KING HENRY The morning's dawn has summon'd me away;
Now, Richard, wake in all the hells of guilt;
And let that wild despair, which now does prey
Upon thy mangled thoughts, alarm the world.
Awake, Richard, awake to guilty minds
A terrible example.
GLOUCESTER Give me a horse – bind up my wounds!
Have mercy, Heav'n! Ha! Soft! 'twas but a dream;
But then so terrible, it shakes my soul:
Cold drops of sweat hang on my trembling flesh;
My blood grows chilly, and I freeze with horror;
Oh tyrant Conscience! How dost thou afflict me?
When I look back, 'tis terrible retreating:
I cannot bear the thought, nor dare repent.

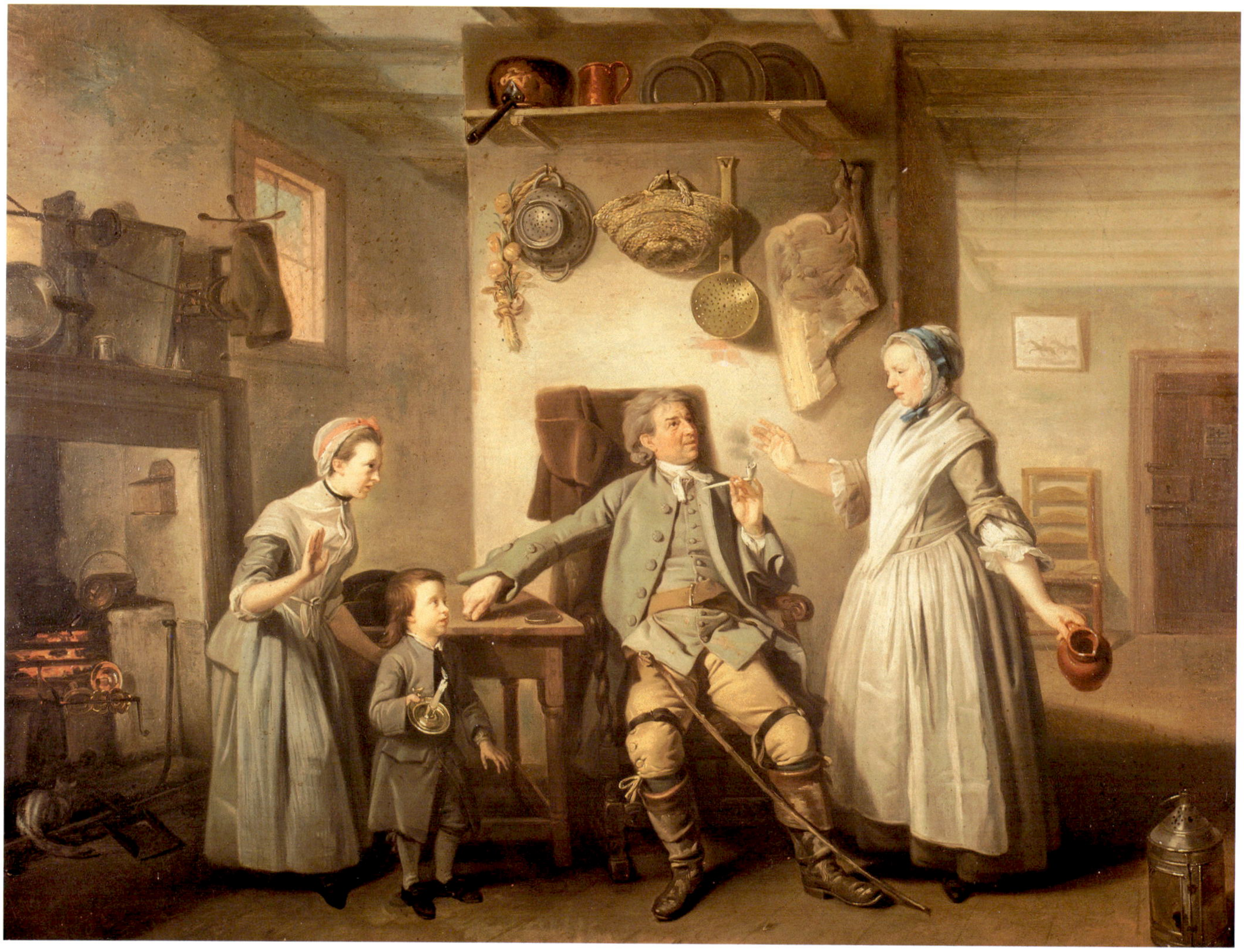

Cat. 14 Johan Zoffany, *David Garrick in 'The Farmer's Return'*, Lambton Trustees.

Hogarth conveys the spiritual self-destruction of a guilty soul: Richard clutches at a dagger and holds the blade, which must surely give him a self-inflicted wound and mean that he has really and symbolically 'blood on his hands'; he turns his back on a carved crucifix – the image of his salvation. As Arthur Murphy's description makes clear, the climax of the scene came with Cibber's (not Shakespeare's) words 'Have mercy, heav'n!' The power of the painting lies in its combination of the literal fact of a portrait with its intimation of the Shakespearean 'inward man' (in Murphy's phrase).

One of Garrick's pet subjects was the happy marriage. He was himself happily married and was sometimes teased for his uxoriousness; he often treated the subject, as in his *Farmer's Return* (cat. no. 14). Hogarth also wanted to celebrate happy marriage after the success of his supremely unhappy *Marriage à la Mode*. He sketched a *Wedding Dance* (Tate) and a *Wedding Banquet* (cat. no. 52) for the new series, but somehow lost interest in such an undramatic subject. David Garrick bought the *Wedding Banquet* and wrote, in collaboration with George Colman, *The Clandestine Marriage* (1766), which in some sense realises Hogarth's project for him – as he says in the prologue 'your matchless Hogarth gives the thought'. Hogarth's other 'happy marriage' is the double portrait of David and Eva Maria Garrick (fig. 4) of 1757, which has exactly the character of one of Garrick's short interludes – it might be called *The Matrimonial Muse*. The original idea is to parody those heroic portraits where a writer attends to the dictates of his Muse, only in this mock-heroic Eva Maria tiptoes up behind

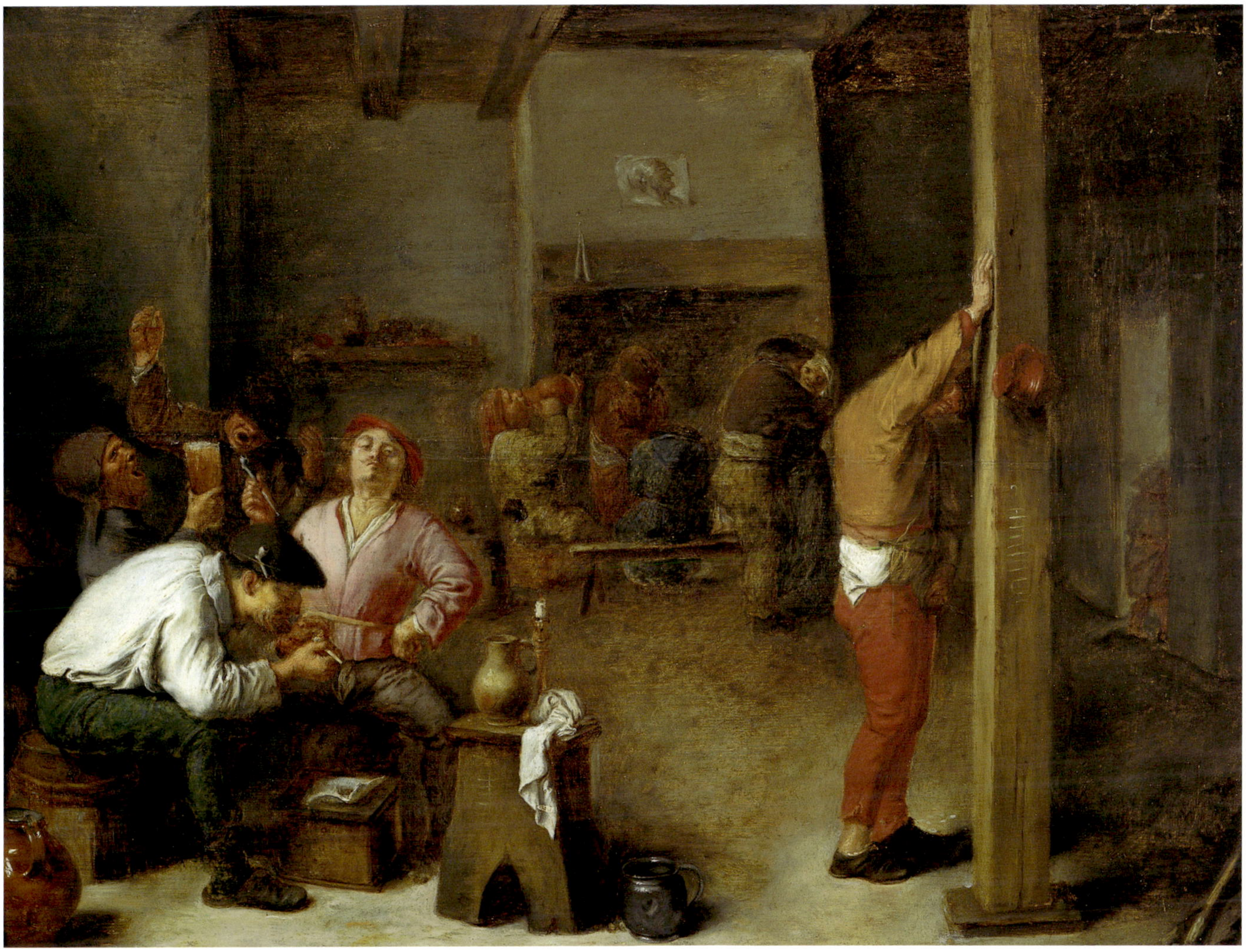

Fig. 7 Adrien Brouwer (1695/6–1638)
Interior of a Tavern, oil on panel, 32.4 × 43.2 cm, Dulwich Picture Gallery.

Garrick's chair and attempts to snatch away his quill while he is musing. In this scene of light raillery we cannot decide whether Eva Maria is a nuisance or an inspiration. A letter written by John Hoadly exactly evokes the subject and the tone of the painting:

> David is sitting at a table, smilingly thoughtful over an epilogue . . . his head supported by his writing-hand; and Madam is archly enough stealing away his pen unseen behind. It is not so much fancy as to be affected or ridiculous and yet enough to raise it from the formal inanity of a mere portrait.[41]

It was not until the 1750s that Garrick seems to have wished to record his performances in any systematic way. The artist he found to do this was one Benjamin Wilson (1721–1788), who was well able to record the rather makeshift appearance of the Georgian Theatre, but not the power of Garrick's performance (see cat. no.s 8, 13 and 28). Garrick was perfectly aware of Wilson's limitations: he wrote in 1757 to Hogarth, '*Wilson* is not an Accurate Observer of things, not Ev'n of those which concern him most'.[42] Fortunately for Garrick in 1762 he encountered a young German assistant in Wilson's studio, with talents far exceeding his master. Garrick's commissions enabled Johan Zoffany (1733–1810) to set up on his own, and launched his career as the greatest theatrical painter ever. Zoffany has two great strengths: a strong, clearly articulated technique and an ability to assimilate any style he likes. Stylistic assimilation (whether pastiche or parody) was also an essential part of the eighteenth-century stage. If we examine Garrick's top ten favourite parts we find that five are Elizabethan or Jacobean: Benedict, Hamlet, Lear and Richard III (see cat. no.s 8 and 13 and fig. 1), from Shakespeare, and Kitely from Jonson's *Every Man in his Humour* (cat. no. 29); four are Restoration: Sir John Brute from Vanbrugh's *The Provok'd Wife* of 1697 (cat. no. 22), Archer from Farquhar's *The Beaux' Stratagem* of 1707, Bayes from Buckingham's *The Rehearsal* of 1671, and Lothario from Nicholas Rowe's *The Fair Penitent* of 1703. Only one is modern: Ranger from Benjamin Hoadly's *The Suspicious Husband* of 1747 (cat. no. 7).[43] These Elizabethan and Restoration plays had to be adapted, to remove their coarse language, incomprehensible jokes and indecent scenes.[44] At the same time new linking scenes had to be introduced in a pastiche of the original style. Davies wrote of Ben Jonson's *Every Man in his Humour*:

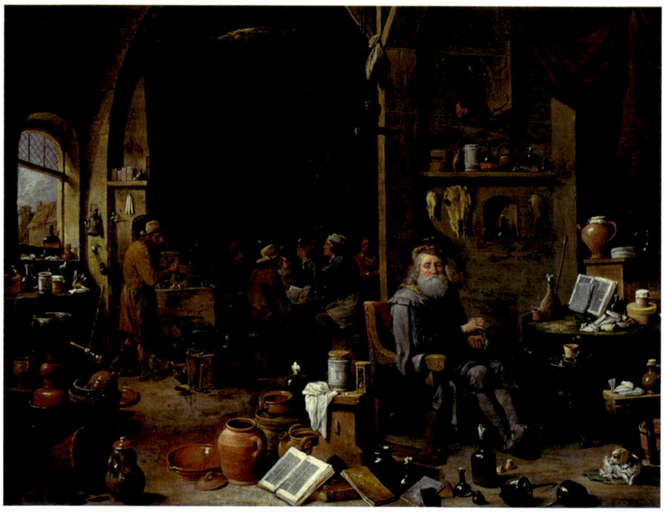

Fig. 8 David Teniers (1610–1690), *An Alchemist in his Laboratory*, *late 1670s*, oil on canvas, 51 × 71 cm
Reproduced by Permission of the Duke of Devonshire and the Chatsworth Settlement Trustees.

> The antiquated phrase of old Ben appeared so strange, and was so opposite to the taste of the audience that he found it no easy matter to make them relish the play. However, by obstinate perseverence, and by retrenching everything that hurt the ear or displeas'd the judgement, he brought it at last to be a favourite dramatic dish, which was then presented to full and brilliant audiences.[45]

Buckingham's *The Rehearsal* is little more than an elaborate literary parody of the extravagant poetry of John Dryden, which depended for its humour upon the audience recognising the source. The play involves the vain playwright, Bayes, rehearsing his absurdly pompous and improbable tragedy. Its success explains Sheridan's re-writing of exactly the same idea in his *The Critic* of 1779. Garrick re-cast Sir John Vanbrugh's *The Provok'd Wife* in 1744, as usual cutting the vulgarity; he also played Sir John Brute in a completely different way from his rival, Quin. Instead of a brutish Brute, Garrick makes him a roguish Brute: one writer describes him as 'such a joyous agreeable wicked dog, that we never think we can have enough of his company, and when he drinks confusion to all order there is scarce a man in the house who is not for that moment a reprobate at heart'. What is striking here is the mixture between 'modern' and 'period' drama, for the character just described sounds like the soul of the Restoration rake, and the audience's enjoyment of the part sounds almost nostalgic. Yet all observers commented that the costumes in the play were satires on the idiocies of modern fashions.[46] Part of the comedy of the brawl scene (cat. no. 22) when Brute is dressed as a woman (he has stolen the clothes from a journeyman tailor in order to give them to his wife) derives from the fact that he has to fight in the absurdly wide and unwieldy hooped skirts then in fashion.[47]

Zoffany realised that theatrical painting must be slightly artificial – it must look like a stage rather than like reality – but without being awkward. He achieves this by introducing a species of visual parody, which exactly matches the literary parodies of the period. Garrick must have warmed to the idea even if he didn't suggest it. His remarks quoted above about acting Abel Drugger end with the words: 'it finishes the compleatest low Picture of *Grotesque Terror* that can be imagin'd by a *Dutch* painter'. This analogy was used elsewhere in the period, as when an actor called Benjamin Johnson was described as 'the Hemskirk or D. Teniers of the theatre; the honest Dutch painter, who contents himself with giving a portrait of mere nature.'[48] What if a theatrical painter could add their own parody of a *Dutch* painter to that of the actor? This is exactly what Zoffany does in his image of Garrick in *The Farmer's Return* of 1762 (cat. no. 14). When

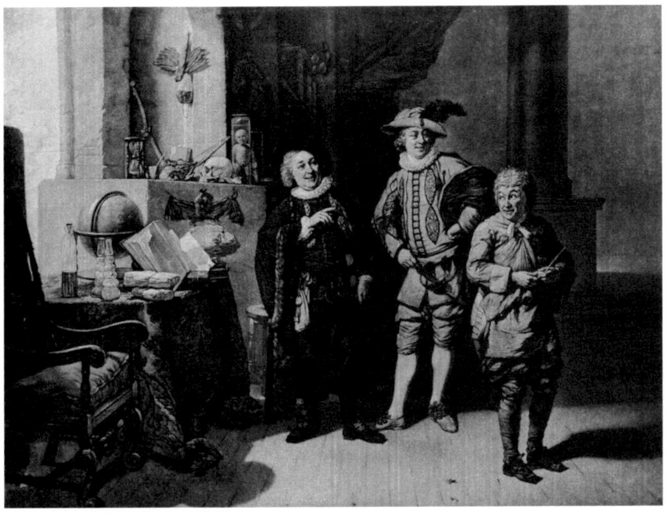

FIG. 9 John Dixon (1740–1811) after Johan Zoffany (1733–1810), *Garrick in the character of Abel Drugger, 1771*, mezzotint engraving, 48 × 60.3 cm
The Lennox-Boyd Collection.

Georgian writers refer to 'low Dutch pictures' they mean the 'Boor's scenes' of Brouwer and Teniers, like that in Dulwich Picture Gallery (fig. 7), though these are in fact Flemish artists. Zoffany has caught the style exactly – the flat stage set, with beams and odd openings, executed in dull greys and browns, and a line of low-life figures disposed across the front, picked out by a cross light, but with only slightly brighter versions of the same colours that occur in the background. The 'Dutch look' probably originated in Hogarth's lost sketch of this moment in the play, which belonged to Garrick and is known through a print (cat. no. 15). Zoffany's skill lies in following Brouwer's technique into details. The moral depends upon the contrast between Brouwer's coarse, drunken, lustful and brawling peasants and Garrick's decent, prosperous, and sober farmer and his good, faithful wife. The other type at which the Flemish excelled were scenes of Alchemists in their laboratories; a characteristic example by David Teniers is at Chatsworth (fig. 8). This is an obvious source for Zoffany's depiction of Ben Jonson's *Alchemist* of 1770 (cat. no 36 and fig. 9) – the spirit of the play and Teniers's painting are extraordinarily close. Hogarth had already parodied Teniers's alchemist subjects in Scene 3 of his *Marriage à la Mode* of 1743–5 (National Gallery, London); Zoffany's parody is even more subtle in the way in which he recycles the obsessively crowded detail of useless clobber, again lit by a cross light, and covered with neat circular highlights, like drops of water. Reynolds bought the original painting (Private Collection) after it was exhibited at the Royal Academy in 1770; it is highly likely that he appreciated the art-historical parody as he himself recommended in his Sixth *Discourse* of 1774 that when it came to Dutch painters 'though they cannot be recommended to be exactly imitated, may yet invite an artist to endeavour to transfer, by a kind of parody, their excellencies to his own performances.'[49] Garrick owned a modest collection of old masters and a superb collection of prints after the old masters: he had the visual sophistication to enjoy these references and others in the work of Zoffany and Reynolds (see below).[50]

Zoffany painted a pair to his *Farmer's Return* in the same year, 1762, showing Garrick as Jaffier and Mrs Cibber as Belvidera in Thomas Otway's famous tragedy of 1681, *Venice Preserv'd* (cat. no.19), a climactic moment in which Jaffier threatens to kill his beloved wife and himself – 'affrighted poor Belvidera is thrown into by Jaffier's drawing his dagger, is succeeded by the bell which announces the execution of Pierre; and makes a fine picture of pity, distress and terror!'[51] This recalls the old masters in a way quite different from its pair. The poses of the figures are fine illustrations of athletic posture of a type that could be learned from Leonardo's treatise (fig. 5); indeed the arrangement of the two figures is a generic quotation from the subject *Noli me Tangere* ('do not touch me'), when the resurrected Christ draws himself away from a kneeling Magdalene, who reaches out towards him. The modern costumes undermine the old master references while the sets seem deliberately to resemble a painted backdrop rather than a 'real' view of Venice.

Artists like Zoffany have the power of being most subtle when they seem at their most simple. No sooner had Garrick discovered Zoffany in Wilson's studio in 1761 than he was inviting him, much to Wilson's disgust, to lodge at his Villa by the Thames at Hampton in order to paint a series of portraits of the house and its owner (cat. no.s 16, 17 and 18). This is Garrick the country gentleman and Zoffany the 'delightfully English' painter of conversation pieces. But Garrick was not a country gentleman and Zoffany was not English. The whole thing is something of a send-up. The models for Zoffany's paintings are those small-scale portraits

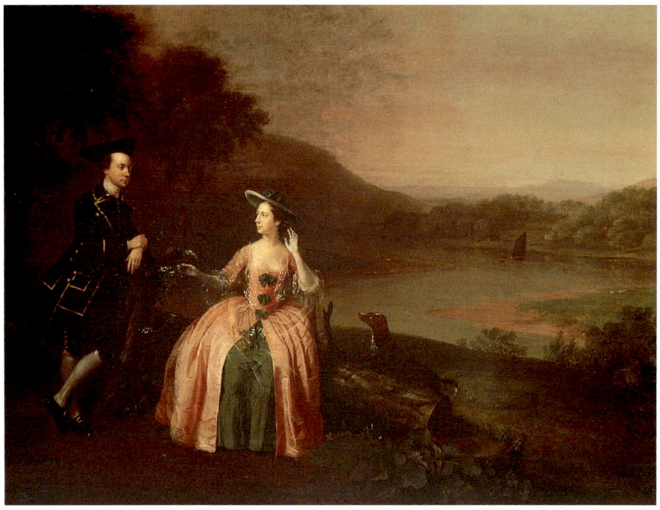

FIG. 10 Arthur Devis (1711–1787), *Sir George and Lady Strickland, 1751* oil on canvas, 91.4 × 115.6 cm, Ferens Art Gallery, Hull City Museums and Art Gallery.

of gentlemen and their families grouped in front of their country estates, executed with doll-like figures and carpets of improbably neat grass by Arthur Devis (1711–1787) (fig. 10). This vogue peaked in the 1740s and early 1750s, when Gainsborough executed some more imaginative examples of the type, like his famous *Mr and Mrs Andrews* (National Gallery, London) of 1748. By 1762 Gainsborough had moved on and the type itself, which had always looked provincial, was beginning to look *passé* as well. It seems impossible that someone as urbane and cultivated as Garrick would choose this genre without a certain amount of tongue in cheek. The analogy here is with the strange mix of modern and old-fashioned which must have been part of the pleasure of Garrick's performances of his Restoration roles (discussed above). Indeed, it seems that he regarded it in exactly the same way: as a form which could be updated, preserving the character of the original while removing the faults that jar – indecency in the case of the comedies, naivety in the case of the paintings. A closer look at the imagery suggests that this is indeed an affectionate parody. The point of Devis's images is to show the Lord of the manor as exactly that – the owner and ruler of his land and of his family. Zoffany shows Garrick and his wife in front of the Temple of Shakespeare, which he built in 1755 (cat. no.16); this is just the sort of thing Devis would have done, but Zoffany shows Mrs Garrick *above* her husband, who stares up at her with an abject devotion. Of course if you stand in front of a Temple of Shakespeare you must become something of a worshipper – your wife becomes a feisty Rosalind and you a lovesick Orlando. No doubt this is what Garrick looked like when Horace Walpole first saw him 'ogling and sighing' at his future wife.[52] The two contrasting dogs (in part presumably symbols of fidelity) and the obviously overheated manservant all add to the comedy. *A View in Hampton Garden with Mr and Mrs Garrick taking tea*, also of 1762 (cat. no.17) is similarly played for laughs, with exaggerated gestures and the slightly absurd suggestion that they are all waiting for Garrick's brother, George, to catch a fish before they can dine.

It is impossible to image a less naïve painter than Zoffany, who was trained in highly wrought continental Baroque style and could move easily between styles. He has caught the situation of the Devis conversation piece – politeness on grass – and some tricks of the Devis 'look' – slightly over-realised figures, in attitudes of exaggerated elegance, against simple blocks of background colour. On the other hand he describes each part with a completely different depth of observation and technique. Perhaps not surprisingly for a theatrical painter the figures have a liveliness and characterisation far beyond anything in Devis (or Hayman and early Gainsborough for that matter). For the luminous landscape executed with a thick and sensual touch he has looked at the most advanced British landscape painter of the day, Richard Wilson, then at the peak of his powers and popularity.[53] Wilson's contemporaneous views of country houses – *Wilton House from the Southeast* of 1758–60 (Private Collection) and *Syon House from Richmond Gardens* of the early 1760s (Neue Pinakothek, Munich) – have the same disposition of grass and water in pleasing blocks of colour. These paintings and the *Banks of the River Dee from Eaton Hall* (Barber Institute, Birmingham), which was exhibited at the Society of Artists in 1760, all have the same effect of hazy summer light suspended in the air.[54]

A love of 'retro' style is perhaps natural for a landed aristocracy, who have (or wish to have) an ancient lineage and history of ownership of their 'patch'. Possibly for this reason Zoffany's reinvention of Arthur Devis caught on and

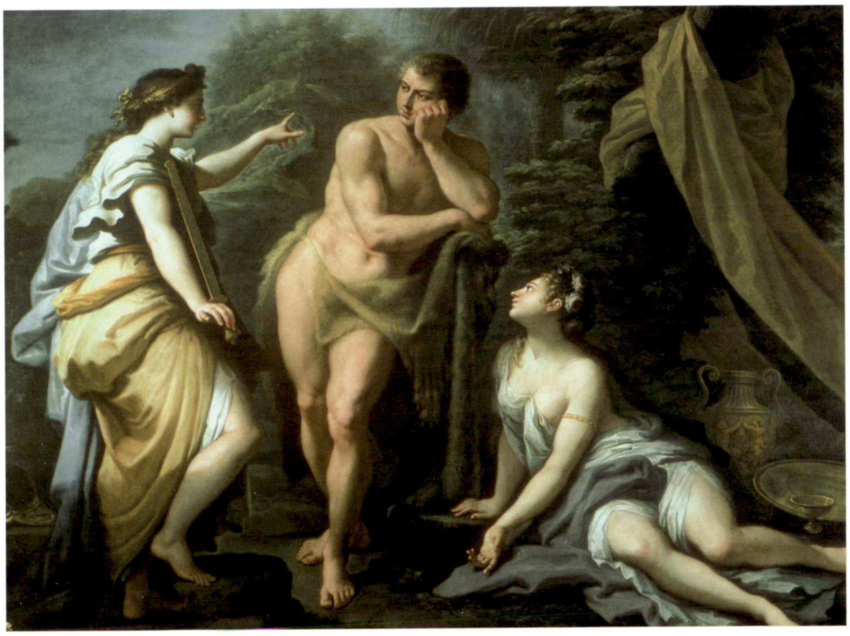

FIG. 11 Paolo de Matteis (1662–1728)
The Choice of Hercules, 1712, oil on canvas, 198.2 × 256.5 cm
Ashmolean Museum, Oxford.

gave the parkland (and interior) conversation piece another decade of life. However Zoffany's conversations always have some element of natural animation or humour and a certain exaggeration of gesture, which belongs with their general character of gentle and affectionate parody.

Garrick must have met Reynolds some time in the 1750s, through their mutual friend Samuel Johnson. It was not until *c.*1760 that they 'worked together' on Reynolds's famous painting *Garrick Between Tragedy and Comedy* (cat. no. 11). By this time Reynolds was a well-established portrait painter with a single comic work to his name – a 1751 caricature of Grand Tourists in Rome in the style of Thomas Patch, arranged as a parody of Raphael's *School of Athens* (National Gallery of Ireland). Though, as we have seen, Reynolds appears to have executed this painting for himself, it was surely Garrick that reawakened his inclination for comedy and parody.

This, Reynolds's most brilliant and ambitious portrait, is a mock-heroic in the tradition Pope's *Rape of the Lock*. One of the characteristics of the mock-heroic form is that it is as widely allusive: you are supposed to be reminded of many different precedents, which the work, to a more or less obvious extent, 'takes off'. The point of such allusiveness is of course that it must be conscious – a reasonable proportion of viewers must have a reasonable chance of getting the joke. Reynolds's challenge to the viewer to 'source hunt' in this case has been eagerly taken up by scholars, to the extent perhaps that the joke has been buried in erudition.[55] It is therefore worth returning to basics of the image. Horace Walpole's description of the painting in 1761, the year it was completed, is a good place to start:

> Reynolds has drawn a large picture of three figures to the knees, the thought taken by Garrick from the judgement of Hercules. It represents Garrick between Tragedy and Comedy. The former exhorts him to follow her exalted vocation, but Comedy drags him away, and he seems to yield willingly, though endeavouring to excuse himself, and pleading that he is forc'd. Tragedy is a good antique figure, but wants more dignity in the expression of her face. Comedy is a beautiful and winning girl – but Garrick's face is distorted, and burlesque.[56]

The subject of the Choice of Hercules comes from a variety of antique literary sources, of which Cicero's *De Officiis* of 44 BC was probably the most accessible and had the advantage too that Joseph Addison paraphrased it in the *Tatler*.[57] Hercules is asked to choose between Pleasure, who offers instant gratification, and Virtue, who offers nothing but labour and difficulty, but with the ultimate reward of honour and justifiable pride. The subject is popular in art and was made more so in England by Shaftesbury's short treatise *A Notion of the Historical Draught or Tablature of the Judgment of Hercules* of 1713, in which Shaftesbury recommends the most eloquent treatment of the subject while at the same time commissioning the Italian artist Paolo de Matteis to realise his conception (Ashmolean Museum) (fig. 11).[58] Shaftesbury and de Matteis follow existing practice in flanking Hercules with a beguiling, sensuous, lazy, softly-coloured figure of Pleasure, and a severe, noble and sensibly-dressed figure of Virtue.

In mock-heroics things need to be sufficiently similar to achieve a match before being turned on their heads. There are many reasons why Comedy and Tragedy are here ideal travesties. Hercules chooses between Virtue and Pleasure (not Vice as is often said): Tragedy is certainly virtuous and Comedy pleasurable. However there is, in this case, no suggestion that the choice is a moral one, so that the earnestness of the original can be turned to innocent fun: Comedy and Tragedy are alternative genres but, in the right hands, they are both sources of moral instruction. This is especially true of Garrick's comic repertoire, which represented a complete repudiation of the licentiousness of Restoration theatre.[59] There were some frankly ribald mock-heroic paintings in the eighteenth century, like Hogarth's mid-1750s sacrilegious image of Sir Francis Dashwood, dressed as Saint Francis and adoring a crucifix with the figure of a naked woman (Private Collection). Reynolds's painting is clearly not of this type: its humour depends upon Garrick sporting playfully rather than improperly with Comedy.

Comedy and Tragedy look at the world in different ways. A tragedy encourages you to struggle against weakness and evil; a comedy on the other hand suggests you to lighten up, guarding instead against joyless severity and prudish hypocrisy. It is easy to see which of these two world-views the painting inhabits: it is obviously a Comedy. This means that it is Tragedy that looks out of place. The point of the original text lies in the idea that Virtue persuades a heroic mind by offering precisely nothing – Duty is its own reward. Looked at from Comedy's perspective, Tragedy similarly has little to offer, unless you like the spectacle of violent death and general misfortune. There may be the distant prospect of a purging through Pity and Terror but we all know that it can seem very distant indeed. Comedy on the other hand offers the instant pleasure of laughter. In Reynolds's painting Tragedy looks impressive rather than beguiling – a fine statuesque figure pointing upwards, with her emblem the dagger stuck in her belt, but at the moment she is bad-tempered and hectoring – Walpole is right that she is wanting in 'dignity in the expression of her face'. It is difficult to have dignity in this situation. Comedy on the other hand is 'a beautiful and winning girl' – with a smile for her audience, a yielding arch of the body and a captivating way with Garrick; she offers instant gratification. This idea of viewing the world of Tragedy through the spectacles of Comedy is as old as comedy itself: Aristophanes's *The Frogs* of 405 BC is a 'Choice of Dionysus' between the two deceased tragedians, Euripides and Aeschylus. This play and others like it are the source for one of Garrick's favourite Farces, *Lethe; or, Aesop in the Shades*, written by him in 1748 and brought up to date throughout his career.

Garrick makes a hopelessly irresolute Hercules and he chooses Pleasure rather than Virtue – which is why Tragedy is so put out. Comedy cheats: instead of using argument fairly she grabs Garrick by his slashed sleeves and drags him off; she is perhaps even tickling him under the ribs. It is already too late for Tragedy to seize his other hand, so that he can at least hear her out. The symbolism of this is clear: laughter is a physical as well as cerebral pleasure, which attacks the rib cage and enforces helpless submission. As Walpole says, 'Comedy drags him away, and he seems to yield willingly, though endeavouring to excuse himself, and pleading that he is forc'd.' Such an explanation also belongs to the world of comedy – to the world of manners, of apologies, social niceties and fine feelings. Hercules does not trouble to apologise to Pleasure for choosing Virtue. Garrick choreographs this comedy of manners – he shrugs, stammers some excuse, laughs, accepts his fate, inclines towards Tragedy but is joined to Comedy at the hip. Scarcely very Heroic. This is the sort of Hercules that agrees with the last person he has spoken to!

Walpole evidently thought that it was Garrick's idea to parody a 'judgement of Hercules', but Reynolds has certainly 'run with the ball', expressing these ideas in a lightly-worn parody of the heroic language of the old masters. The figure of Tragedy is a 'a good antique figure', painted in what Reynolds would later call the 'Grand Manner' – sculptural, modelled strongly in light and dark, and coloured in simple but sober masses. Comedy is a parody of Correggio, the most pleasing of the old masters, whose speciality was softness, femininity and a certain trade-mark impish smile.

Reynolds never again attempted anything like his 'Choice of Garrick'. However, according to his biographer James Northcote, he did plan in 1772 another ambitious multi-figure composition with Garrick 'in a great many different characters', appearing in 'his proper character in the middle, speaking a prologue'.[60] The idea of this portrait is clearly to celebrate the variety of Garrick's acting, but also the effectiveness of his management. The most obvious expression of this is the prologue – Garrick's formal introduction of himself to his audience at the beginning of every evening's entertainment. Remembering that this usually involved a main play *and* an after-piece, we should probably think of the prologue as functioning rather like a television presenter 'fronting' the 'Garrick Master Theatre Show'.[62] When he speaks his prologue Garrick is author, adaptor, manager as well as actor – it is not surprising that in Reynolds's planned painting the other characters were to be shown 'hearkening to him', presumably in attitudes to reflect their different characters. We don't know why Reynolds abandoned this project, but soon afterwards he painted the famous 'Prologue Portrait' of Garrick (exhibited at the Royal Academy in 1776 and now at Knole), showing him smiling at the viewer from his writing desk, while at work on a prologue.[62] This was one of a set of portraits of intellectuals acquired by the 3rd Duke of Dorset for his 'Chamber of Poets' at Knole: it is interesting that Johnson and Goldsmith are presented in grave and contemplative profile in contrast to the affable and communicative Garrick.

A pattern emerges when examining Garrick's relation with 'his' artists: he finds established painters (or painters of obvious proficiency) and helps them to venture outside their normal patch. He gives Hogarth a 'leg up' into history painting, he tempts Reynolds into mock-heroic comedy, and he sets Zoffany up as a master of the glancing parody. He tried it once more with an artist of sprightly temperament, ideally suited as friend and collaborator: Thomas Gainsborough (1727–1788). Like Reynolds, Gainsborough was in his mid-thirties when he met Garrick (in the early 1760s); he had recently moved to Bath from Suffolk (in 1759), where he had built from scratch a new career as a painter of life-size portraits. This was a time when public exhibitions (amongst many other factors) were making portrait painters think more ambitiously about the subject matter of their work – the ideas and 'stage business', as opposed to mere likeness. In this respect Gainsborough was very slow off the mark: by 1768 (the date of the foundation of the Royal Academy) he had produced nothing but uncomplicated portraits. The nearest he came to symbolism or narrative were a portrait of his daughters with the attributes of painting (*c.*1763, Worcester Art Museum, Massachusetts) and a portrait of his friend's wife, Ann Ford, with an assemblage of musical 'props' (1760, Cincinnati Art Museum). His image of James Quin with a bust of Shakespeare (1762-1763, National Gallery of Ireland) has also a certain intellectual liveliness. But what are these to compare with Reynolds's *Garrick between Tragedy and Comedy* (cat. no. 11), or *Mrs Abington as the Comic Muse* (1764, National Trust, Waddesdon Manor), or indeed *Lady Sarah Bunbury Sacrificing to the Graces* (1762, Art Institute of Chicago)? It was around this time that Garrick approached him to produce a full-length of *Shakespeare between Comedy and Tragedy*, probably for Stratford and probably in preparation for Garrick's *Shakespeare Jubilee* of 1769. It should have been a Godsend; it was in fact a disaster.[63] Garrick's face was so lively it was impossible to fix it; Shakespeare's on the other hand was famously vacant – at least according to the only surviving portraits. In August 1768 Gainsborough wrote to Garrick, 'Shakespeare shall come forth forthwith as the Lawyer says – damn the Original Picture of him *with your leave*. For I think a Stupider Face I never beheld'. He goes on to explain his plan, which is to take Shakespeare's appearance from

> his Pictures & Statues just enough to preserve his likeness *past the doubt of all blockheads*, at first sight, and supply a *Soul* from his Works – it is impossible that such a Mind, and Ray of Heaven, could shine, with such a Face & pair of Eyes as that picture has.[64]

This evidently didn't work, because on 22 August 1768 he is writing:

> I have been several days rubbing in & rubbing out my design for Shakespeare and damn me if I think I shall let it go or let you see it at last – I was willing like an Ass as I am, to expose

myself a little, out of the simple Portrait way, and had a notion of shewing where that inimitable Poet had his Ideas from, by an immediate Ray darting upon his Eye turn'd up for the purpose.[65]

Gainsborough is making a bit of a meal of something which others managed quite easily: in 1758 Roubiliac made a perfectly lively full-length marble of Shakespeare for Garrick's temple (which Garrick himself bequeathed to the British Museum), based on the same bust in Trinity Church, Stratford, which Gainsborough calls a 'silly smiling thing', and at about the same time Giovanni Battista Cipriani (1727–1785) created a spectacular image of Shakespeare striding through a stormy landscape, book and pen in hand, for the music room of Henry Dawkins at Standlynch House, commissioned in 1766.[66] In the end Gainsborough gave up and in 1774 painted his portrait of Johann Christian Fischer (Royal Collection) over the aborted Shakespeare, which remained thus hidden until discovered by x-rays and recognised by Martin Postle. Stratford had to be content with Gainsborough's full-length portrait of Garrick with a bust of Shakespeare (see cat. no.s 33 and 34), which was given to the town Council by the sitter in 1769 and was destroyed by the fire in Stratford Town Hall in 1946. Gainsborough did not again to expose himself 'out of the simple Portrait way' for Garrick or anyone else. But he did create a small group of portraits of creative friends, which show their inspiration through the use of light, made to fall like divine illumination, or, in Gainsborough-speak, like 'an immediate Ray' darting down upon their eye 'turn'd up for the purpose'. Gainsborough's portraits of the composers Johann Christian Fischer (1774, Royal Collection) and Carl Friedrich Abel (1777, Huntington Library, San Marino), and the playwright and Garrick collaborator George Colman (*c.* 1775, National Portrait Gallery) are some of his crowning achievements; it is possible that he would not have attempted their sprightly, spirited (if not exactly *spiritual*) character without Garrick's input and the 'Shakespeare episode'.

Gainsborough realised that his strength was likeness – that pleasure of recognition, which is such a fundamental part of portraiture. For Gainsborough, likeness was a delicate flavour which brilliant handling could enhance, but which 'poetic invention' and any other kind of theoretical machinery would destroy. The difference between one artist and another for Gainsborough was 'real performance' not 'genius or conception'.[67] It is amazing to read that, by his own account, this quality of likeness was so volatile that he was unable to preserve it in a copy by his own hand of his portrait of David Garrick (cat. no. 38).[68] This image is such a perfect example of the 'communicating portrait'- a type used equally for friends, acknowledging each other, and for writers (and actors) engaging with their audience – that it is fascinating to listen to Gainsborough's advice as to how it should be hung: 'a Word to the Wise;' he wrote to Garrick in 1772:

if you let your Portrait hang up so high, only to consult your Room, and to insinnuate somthing over the other Door, it never can look without a hardness of Countenance and the Painting flat: it was calculated for breast high & will never have its Effect or likeness otherwise.[69]

Many other artists had sought this 'insinuating' effect: Reynolds (in his 'Prologue' portrait at Knole), Angelica Kauffmann (cat. no. 26) and even Pompeo Batoni (cat. no. 25): but none carried it off with such a natural ease.

This ethos of domestic intimacy was soon to disappear from painting and from the theatre. In the following year Gainsborough quarrelled with the Royal Academy over the hanging of his pictures and only exhibited there again in the six years between 1777 and 1783. Over the next fifty years the two major London theatres transformed themselves from 'playhouses for hearers' into 'theatres for spectators'. These are the words of the playwright, Richard Cumberland, writing in 1806; he goes on to describe how Garrick's acting would be wasted on the 'modern stage' in a way that recalls Gainsborough's feelings about his portrait:

On the stage of the Old Drury in the days of Garrick the moving brow and penetrating eye of that marvellous actor came home to the spectator. As the passions shifted, and were by turns reflected from the mirror of his expressive countenance, nothing was lost; upon the scale of Modern Drury many of the finest touches of his art would necessarily fall short.[70]

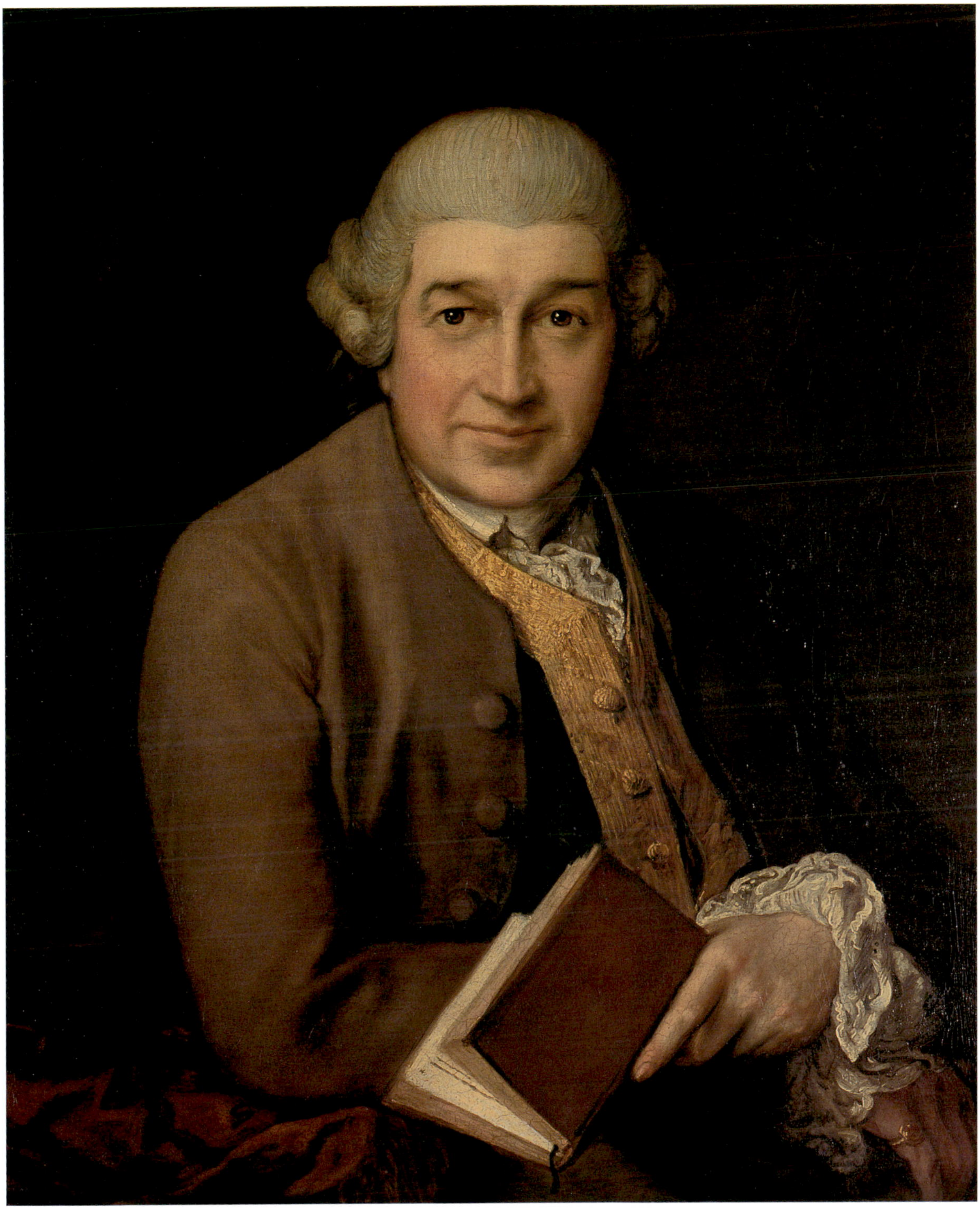

CAT. 38 Thomas Gainsborough, *Portrait of David Garrick*,
Private Collection.

1. Colley Cibber, *An Apology for the Life of Mr. Colley Cibber, Comedian … With an Historical View of the Stage during his Own Time. Written by Himself*, 1740, p. 60.
2. Horace Walpole, *Correspondence with Sir Horace Mann*, 1740–1789, 11 vols., ed. W. S. Lewis et. al., New Haven 1954–71, VI, p. 164.
3. D. M. Little and G. M. Kahrl (eds.) *The Letters of David Garrick*, 3 vols., Cambridge Mass. 1963, p. 419.
4. G. W. Stone and G. M. Kahrl, *David Garrick, A Critical Biography*, London and Amsterdam 1979, p. 296; and see below, cat. no. 6.
5. Stone and Kahrl, p. 303.
6. David Mannings, *Sir Joshua Reynolds: a Complete Catalogue of his Paintings*, 2 vols., New Haven and London 2000, no. 707, p. 212.
7. See Desmond Shawe-Taylor, *The Georgians: Eighteenth-Century Portraiture and Society*, London 1990, Chapters 4 and 7; Hugh Belsey, *Love's Prospect: Gainsborough's Byam Family and the eighteenth-century marriage portrait* (exhibition catalogue, Holburne Museum), Bath 2001.
8. *The Idler* no. 45, 1759.
9. Gary Schwartz, *Rembrandt His Life, His Paintings*, Harmondsworth 1985, p. 96.
10. See below, cat. no.s 5 and 39.
11. See below, cat. no. 7.
12. Letter to Garrick of 22 June 1772 in John Hayes (ed.), *The Letters of Thomas Gainsborough*, New Haven and London 2001, no. 62, p. 105; see also Susan Sloman, *Gainsborough in Bath*, New Haven and London 2002, p. 69.
13. For books in Garrick's library on medals and gems, see Stone and Kahrl, p. 450.
14. Jonathan Richardson, *An Essay on the Theory of Painting*, 1725, p. 209; see also Shawe-Taylor, p. 53.
15. See Shawe-Taylor, pp. 53–8 for a discussion of this type of portrait.
16. Letter from Paris 20 November 1764, reproduced in facsimile in Christopher Lennox-Boyd, G. Shaw, S. Halliwell, *Theatre: in the Age of Garrick. English mezzotints from the collection of the Hon. Christopher Lennox-Boyd* (exhibition catalogue, Courtauld Institute Galleries), London 1994, p. 53.
17. See below, cat. no.s 14, 19 and 22.
18. See below, cat. no. 5.
19. Mannings I, no. 700, p. 209.
20. See below, cat. no 26.
21. See Desmond Shawe-Taylor, *Genial Company: The Theme of genius in Eighteenth-Century British Portraiture*, (exhibition catalogue, Nottingham University Art Gallery and Scottish National Portrait Gallery), Nottingham 1987, no. 23, pp. 28–31.
22. *The Morning Chronicle*, August 1788.
23. See Ronald Paulson, *Hogarth*, Cambridge 1992, II, p.250.
24. The chair is now at the Folger Shakespeare Library, see *Apollo*, July 1972, p. 47.
25. James Boaden (ed.), *the Private Correspondence of David Garrick with the most Celebrated Persons of his Time*, 2 vols., London 1831, II, p. 128.
26. *Letters of David Garrick*, ed. Little and Kahrl, no.s 33 and 47.
27. Letter to Hayman, 10 October 1745.
28. John Adolphus, *Memoirs of John Bannister, Comedian*, London 1839, I, pp. 30–31.
29. 'A Memoir of David Garrick Esq', *The Universal Magazine*, October 1776, p. 187.
30. *The Gentleman's Magazine*, October 1742, quoted in *The Georgian Playhouse* (exhibition catalogue, Hayward Gallery/Arts Council), London 1975, p. 23.
31. Stone and Kahrl, p. 311.
32. Letter of 30 November 1775, in Georg Christoph Lichtenburg, *Lichtenberg Visits to England*, trans. and ed. M. L. Ware and W. H. Quarrell, Oxford 1938 pp. 25–27
33. David Garrick, *An Essay on Acting*, London 1744.
34. Letter of 1 Oct 1775, in *Lichtenberg's Visits to England*, pp. 3–4.
35. *The London Chronicle*, March 1757, quoted in Christopher Lennox-Boyd, G. Shaw, S. Halliwell, *Theatre: in the Age of Garrick. English mezzotints from the collection of the Hon. Christopher Lennox-Boyd*, (exhibition catalogue, Courtauld Institute Galleries), London 1994, p. 61.
36. Stone and Kahrl, p. 13.
37. Joseph Warton, *Essay on the Writings and Genius of Pope*, 1756, I, p. 123.
38. See Martineau et. al., *Shakespeare in Art* (exhibition catalogue, Dulwich Picture Gallery), London 2003, no.s 1 and 2; Ronald Paulson, *Hogarth: His Life, Art, and Times*, 2 Vols., London 1971, II, pp. 343–4.
39. Iain Mackintosh and Geoffrey Ashton, *Thirty Different Likenesses: David Garrick in portrait and performance* (exhibition catalogue, Buxton Museum and Art Gallery), Buxton 1981, p. 1.
40. Joseph Warton, *Essay on the Writings and Genius of Pope*, I, p. 122, quoted in Stone and Kahrl, p. 104.
41. John Hoadley to Joseph Warton, 21 April 1757.
42. Paulson II, p. 234–5, also quoted in Stone and Kahrl, p. 101.
43. Stone and Kahrl p. 656.
44. See Stone and Kahrl, pp. 285–9.
45. *Thirty Different Likenesses: David Garrick in portrait and performance* (exhibition catalogue, Buxton Museum and Art Gallery), Buxton 1981.
46. *The London Chronicle*, 14 October 1758.
47. By 1776 he was wearing a type of cap with plumed feathers, which was *then* in fashion.
48. Thomas Davies, *Dramatic Miscellanies*, 1783–4, III, p. 135.
49. Sir Joshua Reynolds, *Discourses on Art*, ed. Robert R. Wark, San Marino 1975, p. 110.
50. See Stone and Kahrl pp. 449–50 and p. 457.
51. Thomas Davies, *Dramatic Miscellanies*, 1783–4, III, p. 231.
52. See below, cat. no. 9.
53. Garrick himself owned an unidentified Richard Wilson, see Stone and Kahrl, p. 457.
54. David Solkin, *Richard Wilson: The Landscape of Reaction* (exhibition catalogue, Tate Gallery), London 1982, no.s 81a, 83 and 93.
55. Mannings I, no. 700, pp. 209–210, provides an excellent summary of the literature.
56. Horace Walpole, *Book of Materials*, quoted in Mannings I, p. 209.
57. Cicero *De Officiis*, I, xxxiii; Addison, *Tatler*, No. 97, November 22, 1709; Mannings I, p. 209, also draws attention to Xenophon's *Memorabilia*, which contains the story and is of course a more venerable source than Cicero.
58. See Edgar Wind, 'Hume and the Heroic Portrait' in *Studies in Eighteenth-Century Imagery*, ed. Jaynie Anderson, Oxford 1986, pp. 65–6 and 69.
59. See Stone and Kahrl, pp. 285–9.
60. See below, cat. no. 29; Little and Kahrl, p. 419; Shearer West, *The Image of the Actor*, London 1991, p. 42.
61. Stone and Kahrl p. 206 estimates that after-pieces were performed after the main play in eighty percent of evenings at Drury Lane.
62. Mannings I, no. 705, p. 211.
63. The episode is recounted by Martin Postle in 'Gainsborough's "lost" picture of Shakespeare', *Apollo*, December 1991, pp. 374–79.
64. Hayes, *Letters of Thomas Gainsborough*, no. 35, p. 58.
65. Hayes, *Letters of Thomas Gainsborough*, no. 36, p. 60.
66. Martineau et. al., *Shakespeare in Art* (exhibition catalogue, Dulwich Picture Gallery), London 2003, pp. 200–1.
67. See his letter to John Henderson of 18 July 1773, Hayes, *Letters of Thomas Gainsborough*, no. 69, pp 117–8.
68. See Hayes, *Letters of Thomas Gainsborough*, no. 62, p. 105.
69. Hayes, *Letters of Thomas Gainsborough*, no. 63, p. 108.
70. Richard Cumberland, *Memoirs*, 1806, quoted in *The Georgian Playhouse*, p. 221.

PORTRAITS OF DAVID GARRICK

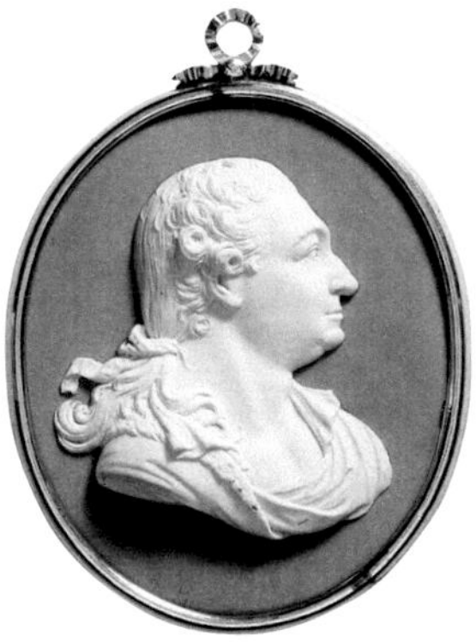

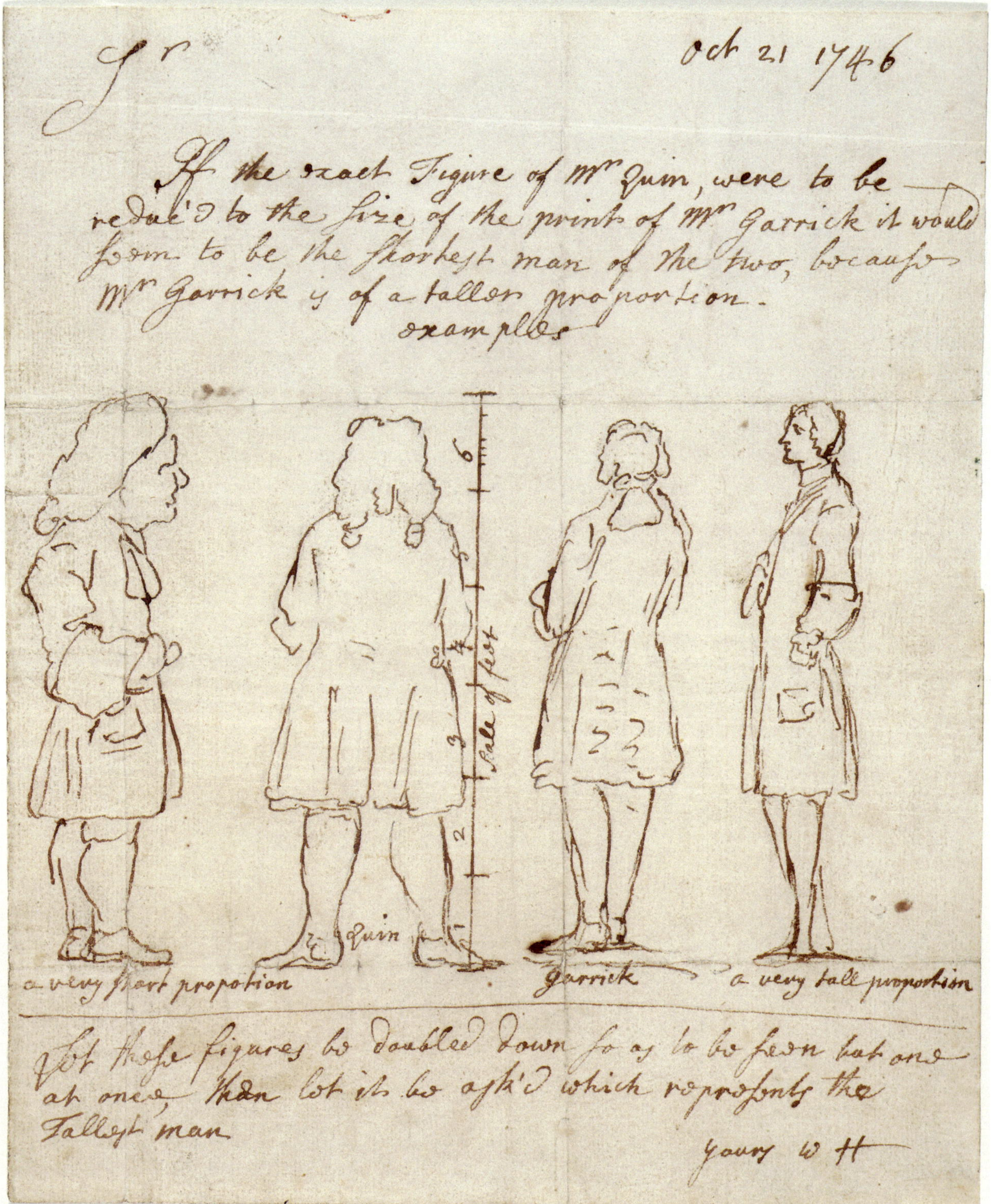

Sr Oct 21 1746

If the exact Figure of Mr Quin, were to be reduc'd to the size of the print of Mr Garrick it would seem to be the shortest man of the two, because Mr Garrick is of a taller proportion.

examples

Let these figures be doubled down so as to be seen but one at once, then let it be ask'd which represents the Tallest man

yours W H

5 **William Hogarth,** *The Proportions of Garrick and Quin*

CATALOGUE

*

ROSIE BROADLEY
with COLIN HARRISON, SUSAN SLOMAN, LISA WHITE
AND CHRISTOPHER WOODWARD

1 **Unknown engraver after Thomas Bardwell (1704–1767)**
***David Garrick as Richard III**, c. 1741*
Engraving, 16 × 12.5 cm
Private Collection

Richard III was the role which launched David Garrick's career in 1741, when he acted in Shakespeare's play at Goodman's Fields theatre and was billed as 'a gentleman, (who never appeared on any Stage)'. The earliest known portrait of Garrick is by Bardwell (Russell-Cotes Art Gallery, Bournemouth), and was made soon after Garrick's debut. Another version of the painting was in the collection of the Duke of Clarendon, when it was engraved by J. Ogborne in 1810. There is also a version recorded as being at Mottisfont Abbey in Hampshire in 1979, as one of the collection of theatrical paintings in the long gallery; its current whereabouts is unknown.[1]

Bardwell was a decorative artist and portrait painter based in East Anglia. He visited London during the 1740s, when it is possible he saw Garrick act. Bardwell also wrote on artistic technique, publishing *The Practice of Painting and Perspective made Easy* in 1756. RB

2 **Bartholomew Dandridge**
David Garrick as Richard III
By courtesy of the Trustees of the Samuel Johnson Birthplace Museum.

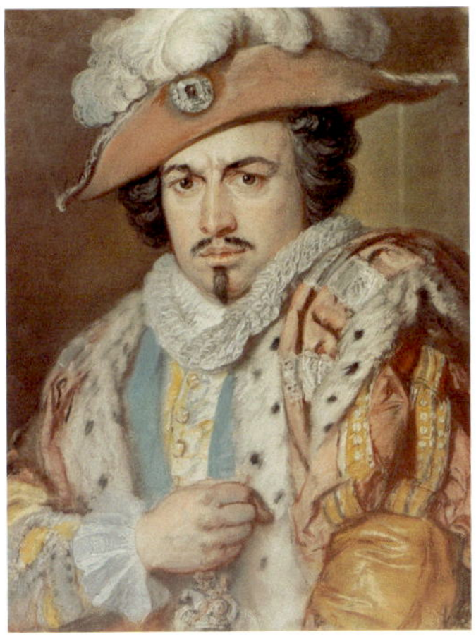

2 **Bartholomew Dandridge (1691–*c.* 1755)**
***David Garrick as Richard III**, c. 1741*
Pastel, 60 × 45 cm
By courtesy of the Trustees of the Samuel Johnson Birthplace Museum

Dandridge has not depicted Garrick in a specific scene in *Richard III*, but rather shows emotional turmoil through facial expression, a device Garrick employed so effectively on stage. This pastel bears similarities to Bardwell's painting in terms of composition and expression, and was made soon after Garrick's famous debut in the role.

Dandridge lived and worked in London, taking over the studio of the society portraitist Sir Godfrey Kneller in 1731. Dandridge was a member of the St. Martin's Lane set of artists, which also included Hogarth and Hayman, and was probably acquainted with Garrick when he arrived in London. RB

1. Heinz Archive and Library, National Portrait Gallery, June 2003.

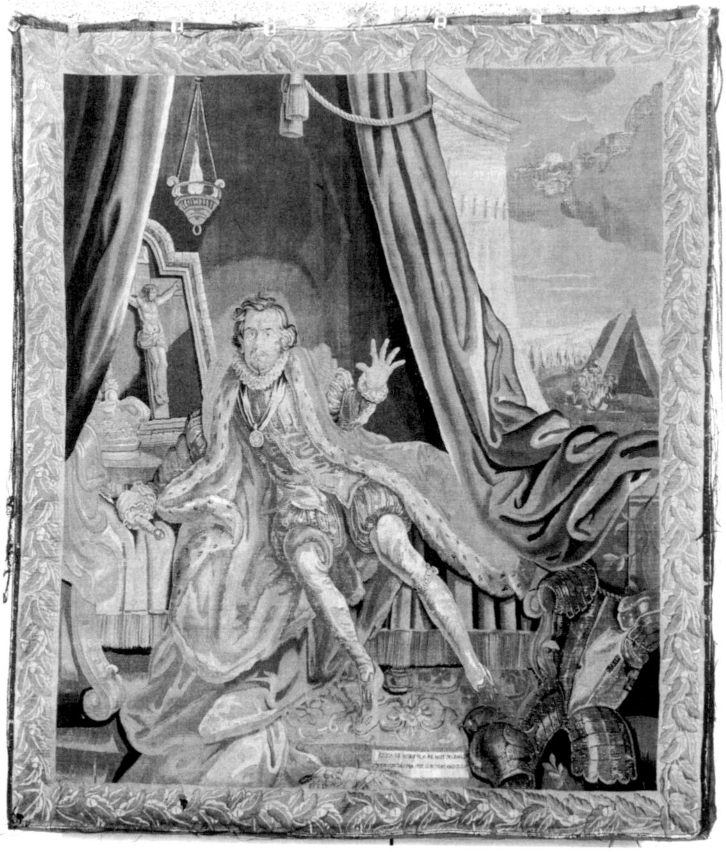

3 **Tapestry portraying David Garrick in the character of Richard III**
The Museum of London.

3 English (Soho, London), after William Hogarth (1697–1764)

Tapestry portraying David Garrick in the character of Richard III, 1746–50
Wool and silk, 183 × 157 cm
The Museum of London

This tapestry derives from Hogarth's famous portrait of Garrick as *Richard III* (Walker Art Gallery, Liverpool), which shows Act V scene III, when Gloucester (later, King Richard) wakes suddenly from a dream, having been visited by the ghosts of each of his victims, including his wife Lady Anne and the young Princes in the Tower.

> Have mercy, Jesu! Soft! I did but dream.
> O! coward conscience, how dost thou afflict me.

The inscription at his feet reads:

> Jockey of Norfolk, be not so bold,
> For Dickon thy master is bought and sold.

This is the ominous wording of the scroll, intended for the Duke of Norfolk, which Richard dismisses later in the same scene, before entering the battlefield for the last time.

The colours of the tapestry vary from the original painting, indicating that its maker did not refer to the painting itself, and the design is most likely to have been taken from the engraving by Hogarth and Charles Grignion (cat. no. 4). The composition has been reversed, and changed from landscape to portrait format, indicating that it was made to fit a specific location, possibly an overmantel. Large tapestries were, by this time, rather old-fashioned forms of decoration. Nevertheless, the tapestry would have been expensive, and was probably commissioned by a wealthy Garrick enthusiast. There are further alterations to smaller details of the original picture, and the tapestry has been surrounded by an oak leaf border.

The tapestry has been ascribed to the group of makers associated with Soho, but has not been attributed to one of the known weavers. However, a similar oak leaf border appears on a Hare Hunt tapestry by William Bradshaw (fl. 1728–75) of Soho Square and Greek Street. He is recorded as having supplied goods to Chevening, Longford Castle and Holkham. RB

4 William Hogarth (1697–1764) and Charles Grignion (1717–1810)

David Garrick in 'Richard III', 1746

Engraving and etching, 46.5 × 56.5 cm

University of Bristol Theatre Collection. Ref TCP/C/000093

INSCRIBED *Painted by W^{m}: Hogarth**** Engrav'd by W^{m}: Hogarth & C. Grignion. / *M^{r}: Garrick* in the *Character* of *Richard* the 3^{d}: / Publish'd according to Act of Parliam^{t}. June 20th. 1746. Shakespear. Act 5. Scene 7

Hogarth's original painting, which is life-size, is considered the greatest theatrical portrait of the eighteenth century (fig. 1). It was bought by Mr Duncombe of Duncombe Hill, Yorkshire, who paid £200 for it, an enormous sum in the early eighteenth century. Hogarth mentions this amount with some pride in his letter to the Argonauts' Society of Norwich (see cat. no. 5): 'more than any other portrait painter was known to receive for a portrait'.

Garrick himself was anxious for a print of this portrait, writing to his friend Somerset Draper to ask him: 'Pray, does *Hogarth* go on with my picture, and does he intend a print from it?'. Both Hogarth and Garrick were aware that the print would raise their profile. Garrick's fame in the role, and the fame of the painting, meant that the print was very successful. The print was still available twenty-five years after it was first published, thanks to Garrick's enduring appeal and his continuing performances as King Richard. Nathaniel Dance and Francis Hayman were to paint Garrick in the same role (see cat. no. 40 and fig.12), but they did not attempt the tent scene, preferring to depict the later scene on Bosworth Field. RB

5 William Hogarth (1697–1764)

The Proportions of Garrick and Quin, 1746

Pen with brown ink, closely following pencil, 22.6 × 36.9 cm

The Royal Collection

Garrick's debut as Richard III in 1741 was the first serious challenge to the pre-eminence of the actor James Quin (1693–1766), who had made his debut in 1715, and who had himself frequently played King Richard. Quin's acting style was declamatory, grandiose and, in the perception of subsequent generations, monotonous. He employed a 'tragic strut'. In contrast, Garrick had developed a naturalistic and energetic style, which caused Quin to remark 'If this young fellow be right, then we have been all wrong'.

This drawing was enclosed in a letter dated 21 October 1746, written by Hogarth to the Argonauts' Society of Norwich, a club for merchants engaged in fabric exporting. The caricature of Quin is labelled 'a very short proportion' and that of Garrick, 'a very tall proportion' and the figures are compared in scale. In reality, Garrick was small and slight and Quin was rotund and imposing. Around the drawing Hogarth has written:

> If the exact Figure of Mr Quin, were to be reduc'd to the size of the print of Mr Garrick it would seem to be the shortest man of the two, because Mr Garrick is of a taller proportion ... If these figures be doubled down so as to be seen but one at once, then let it be asked which represents the tallest man.

Earlier in the same year, Garrick had been concerned that his 'proportion', as described by Hogarth, was increasing. He remarked to his friend Benjamin Hoadly; 'I have been lately allarm'd with some Encroachments of my Belly upon the Line of Grace and Beauty, in short I am growing very fat'. Garrick refers here to Hogarth's developing theories on line and proportion, which would be published as part of Hogarth's treatise *The Analysis of Beauty* in 1753. Hogarth had probably discussed his developing theories with his friends at a house party in the summer of 1746, held by Benjamin's brother the Rev. John Hoadly at his vicarage in Old Alresford, Hampshire, and his ideas had become common currency between the friends.

On the right hand inner page of the letter is another note, in Hogarth's hand, referring to his famous portrait of *Garrick as Richard III* (fig.1):

> The Picture from whence the Print in question was taken, was Painted from M Garrick big as the life, and was sold for two Hundred pounds on account of its Likeness, which was the reason it was call'd Mr. Garrick in the Character of Richard the 3d- and not any body else.

Although the Argonauts' original letter has been lost, Hogarth's response implies that they had obtained a copy of Hogarth's print of this painting, which had been recently published. They were perhaps asking whether the portrait was an accurate likeness. This correspondence shows that Garrick's fame was spreading through prints, even to those who had not seen him act in London. Some of the Argonauts had probably seen Quin act. Could Hogarth's drawing have been prompted by a question of how Garrick compared physically to Quin?

In 1746 Quin and Garrick were both employed at the Covent Garden Theatre. Hogarth was a friend of both actors, and this drawing anticipates a performance of Nicholas Rowe's *The Fair Penitent*, later that year, where the two actors drew swords as Horatio and Lothario. The professional rivalry continued when Garrick took over the management of the Theatre Royal Drury Lane, and Quin remained at Covent Garden. Quin retired to Bath in 1752. The two were reconciled thanks to the intervention of the Duke of Devonshire and, probably, Hogarth. Quin became a frequent guest of the Garricks at Hampton. When Quin died in 1766, Garrick had become sufficiently close to him to be asked to write his epitaph, as he had done for their friend Hogarth, two years previously.

A letter from Garrick to Quin in 1763 reveals that the two actors planned to exchange portraits as 'Tokens of good Will between us'. Garrick had commissioned the artist Thomas Hudson (1701–1779) to paint his portrait, but was having difficulty in arranging an appointment. He was concerned that Hudson had been disheartened by the success of Gainsborough's portrait of Quin, exhibited at the Society of Artists that same year. An engraving by J. Dixon

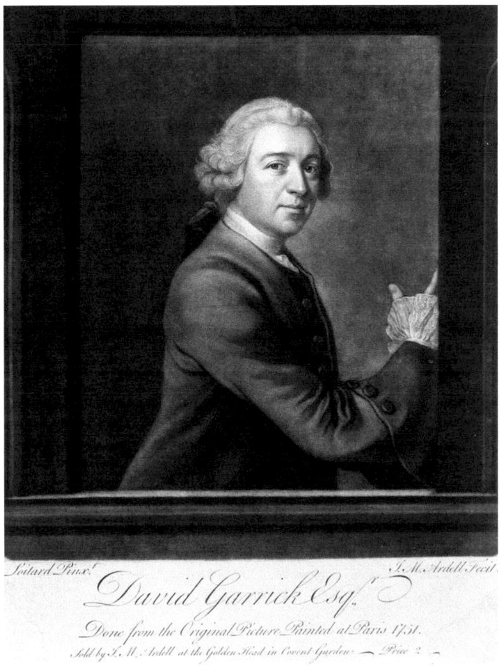

6 **James McArdell**
after Jean-Etienne Liotard
David Garrick
Trustees of the British Museum.

after Hudson of a portrait of Garrick, seated at a table with a book, is dated 1761, but the original portrait has not been traced. Garrick's apologetic tone implies that Quin had already fulfilled his part of the agreement. The only portrait of Quin recorded in Garrick's inventories shows Quin in the character of *Falstaff Reviewing Recruits,* one of several versions painted by Hayman in the 1760s. It may be the portrait that Quin presented to Garrick. RB

6 James McArdell (*c.*1728–1765) after Jean-Etienne Liotard (1702–1789)
***David Garrick**, 1751*
Mezzotint Engraving, 27.5 × 23 cm
Trustees of the British Museum
INSCRIBED *Loitard* [sic] *Pinx.t***J.M.Ardell Fecit. / David Garrick Esq.r /Done from the Original Picture Painted at Paris* 1751. */ Sold by J.M.Ardell at the Golden Head in Covent Garden – Price* 2 –

Garrick and his Austrian wife, the former dancer, Eva Maria Veigel, visited Paris in June 1751. They both sat to the Swiss artist Liotard for portraits in pastel. Garrick appears to have been recommended to visit the studio of the artist, noting in his diary: 'Went to see Leotard's Pictures which are indeed very like'. Obviously impressed, Garrick was himself sitting to Liotard the very next day, and on four further occasions. Garrick also twice dined with Liotard, describing him as 'a very sensible unaffected man, a little vain as they all are'.

Garrick's diary of his trip to Paris demonstrates his enthusiasm for visiting art collections. He had noted down opening times of the gallery at the Palais du Luxembourg in the margin of his diary and, after breakfast on 3 June: 'step'd over to ye Luxembourgh to see a particular closet of pictures which is not to be seen on ye publick days, there we saw all ye work (as ye man told us) of one Guillame Bor'.

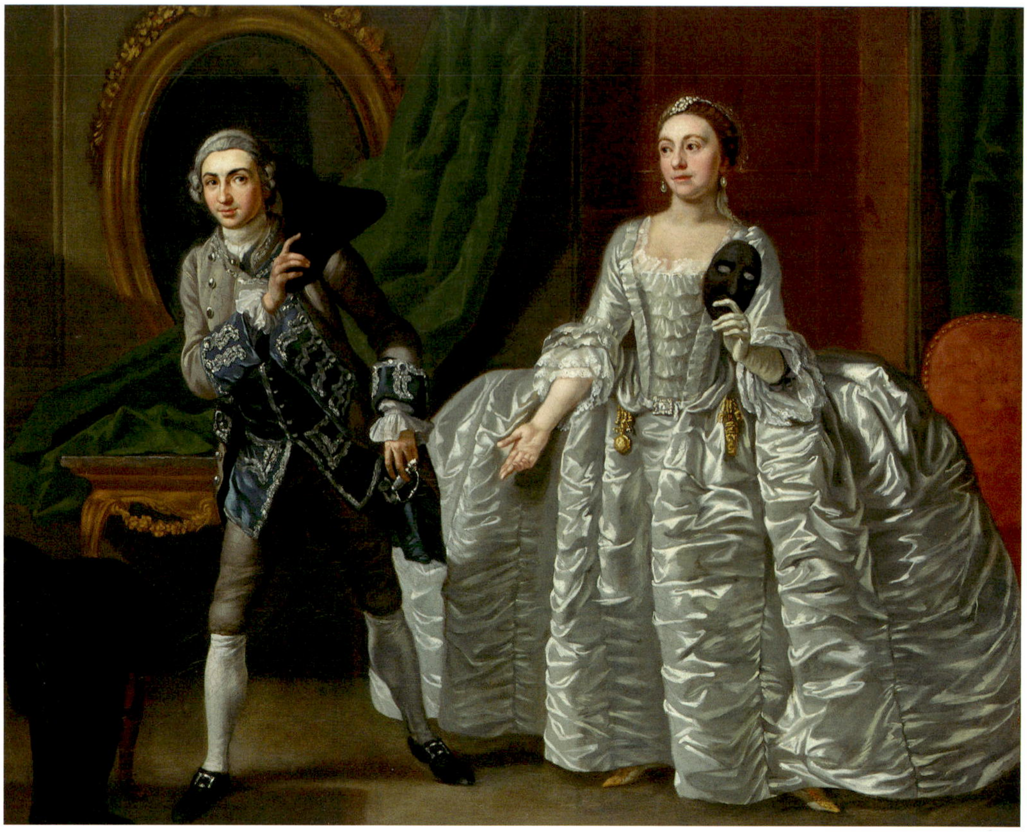

7 **Francis Hayman**
Garrick in 'The Suspicious Husband'
The Museum of London.

Garrick commissioned these two portraits as gifts for the 3rd Earl and Countess of Burlington who had been Mrs Garrick's patrons when she first arrived in England in 1746. Walpole records the pastels as being in Lady Burlington's dressing room at Chiswick House. While Garrick was in Paris, he was all the time comparing the pictures he was seeing in Paris, to the collection at Chiswick, which he had become familiar with as a guest of the Burlingtons: 'No hotel has so good a collection of Pictures as there is at Chiswick, in general Rubbish to 'em'.[2] Much of the Burlingtons' collection was transferred to Chatsworth following the marriage of their daughter Charlotte into the Cavendish family. Garrick's inventory shows that he owned another portrait by Liotard, of his friend Richard Berenger, which hung in Garrick's green dressing room at Hampton

This print is like the pastel now at Chatsworth, but some details differ, including the wig, and the folds of the jacket. A painting of Garrick by Liotard was at one time reported to be at the Burghley Estate, and a copy hangs in the Theatre Royal, Drury Lane.[3] The Chatsworth pastel of Mrs Garrick shows her wearing an elaborate white lace jacket. A portrait of Mrs Garrick by Liotard appears in the 1823 sale of the contents of the villa at Hampton, but she is described as wearing 'a black silk cloak and hat'. It seems likely, therefore, that Garrick had Liotard make two pairs of portraits of himself and his wife, but that he kept a portrait only of Eva Maria to grace his own home, giving away portraits of himself as gifts. RB

2. *The Diary of David Garrick; Being a record of his memorable trip to Paris in 1751*, New York 1971, p. 18.

3. Philip H. Highfill, Kalman A. Burnim and Edward A. Langhans, *A Biographical Dictionary of Actors, Actresses, Musicians... in London 1660–1800*, 16 vols., Carbondale 1973, III, p. 29.

7 Francis Hayman (1708–1776)

Garrick and Mrs Pritchard in Benjamin Hoadly's 'The Suspicious Husband', 1752

Oil on canvas, 71.25 × 91.5 cm

The Museum of London

The painting shows a scene in Act IV of the comedy *The Suspicious Husband*. Garrick, as the rake Ranger, mistakenly believes he is in the company of a woman of doubtful reputation. To his surprise, she unmasks to reveal that she is, in fact, his cousin Clarinda (played by Mrs Pritchard). 'I must brazen it out' says Ranger in an aside. Benjamin Hoadly had written the part of Ranger especially for Garrick. When George II saw Garrick's performance, he laughed so much that he allowed the play to be dedicated to him. *The Suspicious Husband* proved extremely lucrative for Garrick, perhaps explaining why he played Ranger more than any other part: 121 times in total.

Hayman painted two versions of this scene. The first, for Hoadly, was made soon after the first performance and was adapted from a sketch (painting and sketch, Yale Centre for British Art). The extraneous details which Hayman omitted from the final painting (the figure of a maid, and a stool in the right foreground) suggest that the sketch was made during a performance or rehearsal. Garrick commissioned a replica of Hoadly's painting from Hayman in 1752, for which he paid 20 guineas. It does not appear in his inventories, and was perhaps bought as a gift.

Hayman had been working as a scene painter since 1732 at Goodman's Fields Theatre and, from 1736, at the Theatre Royal, Drury Lane. Like Garrick, Hayman was a theatrical innovator; contemporary accounts of his work suggest that he was an early exponent of naturalistic landscape in scenery. He abandoned scenery painting in the mid-1740s. In 1741 Hayman was illustrating Sir Thomas Hanmer's edition of Shakespeare, and his paintings for the supper boxes at Vauxhall Gardens included scenes from modern drama and Shakespeare.

Garrick and Hayman were established friends by 1745. In October, Garrick wrote eagerly to Hayman 'damn all formality between Us. Have you finished My Picture Yet?'. He is referring to the double portrait of Garrick and his friend William Windham of Felbrigg (Private Collection, fig. 2), which Garrick later hung in his dining room at Hampton. The two had been sitting to Hayman that summer, and during sittings the three men had evidently discussed Hayman's planned set of six prints of Shakespearean subjects. Garrick's letter assures Hayman that Windham and himself were doing all they could to secure subscribers for the scheme, and offered advice on how to represent some of these scenes:

> If you intend altering the Scene in Lear...what think You of the following one? Suppose Lear Mad upon the Ground with Edgar by him; His Attitude Should be leaning upon one hand and pointing Wildly towards the Heavens with his Other, Kent & Fool attend him & Glocester comes to him with a Torch; the real Madness of Lear, the Frantick Affectation of Edgar, and the different looks of Concern in the three other Characters will have a fine Effect; Suppose You express Kent's particular Care and distress by putting him upon one Knee begging & entreating him to rise & go with Gloster.

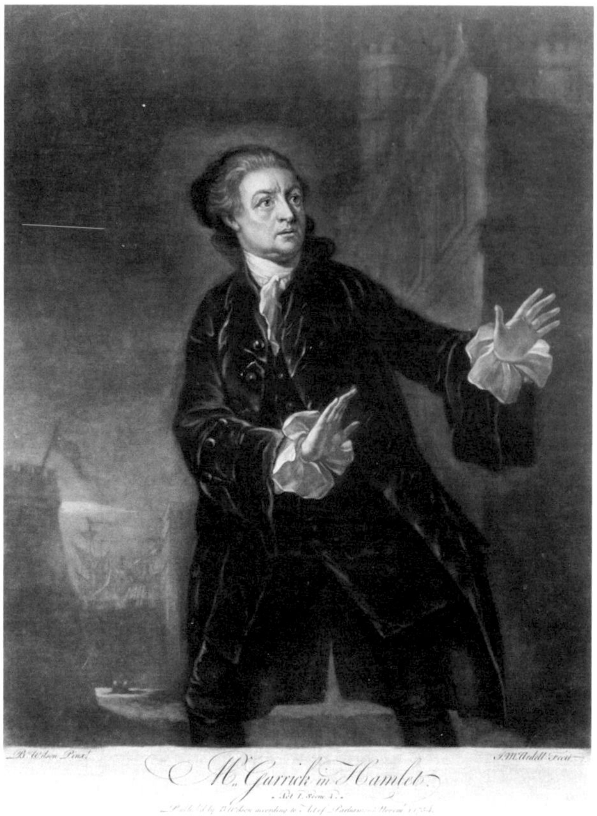

8 **James McArdell after Benjamin Wilson,** *David Garrick as Hamlet,* Trustees of the British Museum.

In a later letter to Hayman, Garrick advises the artist on representing scenes from *Othello*, and suggests that he should personally demonstrate the appropriate attitude for each of the players to be illustrated: 'I shall better make you conceive My Notion of this Attitude & Expression when I see you.' Garrick is directing Hayman to paint the figures, perhaps as he would his cast in rehearsal. Hayman painted Garrick again, as Richard III, after a revival of the play in 1759. This painting was exhibited at the first exhibition of The Society of Artists (Maugham Collection, The National Theatre; fig. 13). RB

8 James McArdell (*c.* 1728–1765) after Benjamin Wilson (1721–1788)

***David Garrick as Hamlet seeing the Ghost**, 1754*

Mezzotint Engraving, 41.25 × 32.5 cm

Trustees of the British Museum

INSCRIBED *B. Wilson Pinx$^{t.}$ ***J. Mc Ardell Fecit. / Mr Garrick in Hamlet. / Act* 1. *Scene* 4. / *Publish'd by B. Wilson according to Act of Parliament Novem.^{r}* 1. st 1754.

Hamlet, played by Garrick, is shown at the moment of confrontation with the ghost of his dead father, the King of Denmark, who has been murdered by his brother Claudius:

What may this mean,
That thou, dead corpse, again in complete steel,
Revisit'st thus the glimpses of the moon, and we fools of nature

So horridly to Shake our disposition
With thoughts beyond the reaches of our souls?
Say, why is this? wherefore? what should we do?

Wilson's representation agrees with Lichtenberg's description of the very specific movements that Garrick had devised, in order to heighten the dramatic effect:

> Garrick turns sharply and at the same moment staggers back two or three paces with his knees giving way under him; his hat falls to the ground and both his arms, especially the left, are stretched out nearly to their full length, with hands as high as his head, the right arm more bent and the hand lower, and fingers apart; his mouth is open; thus he stands rooted to the spot, with legs apart, but no loss of dignity, ... His whole demeanour is so expressive of terror that it made my flesh creep even before he began to speak.[4]

Garrick first played Hamlet in Dublin in 1742, and it became his most frequent tragic role. In the early 1770s Garrick altered the play, restoring over six hundred lines of Shakespeare's original text, which had been lost, adding some lines of his own, and also removing certain scenes. In 1772, he wrote to his French friend, the Abbé Morellet: 'I have dar'd to alter Hamlet, I have thrown away the gravedigger, & all ye 5th Act.' His adaptation was considered a success. The first three productions of this new presentation brought in takings each night of £260, over £100 more than an average full-house. Garrick is said to have been buried with a copy of the play. This is one of the prints Garrick requested his brother send him from Paris. RB

9 Katherine Read (1723–1779)

Mrs Garrick (1724–1822), c. 1755
Oil on canvas, 59 × 47.5 cm
Private Collection

Garrick married the Austrian dancer Eva Maria Veigel in June 1749. Known professionally as Violette, she gave her first performance in London in 1746 at the Opera House in the Haymarket, and proved a great success. 'The fame of the Violetta increases daily' commented Horace Walpole on 6 June. Eva Maria lived under the protection of the Earl and Countess of Burlington in Piccadilly. Lady Burlington was keen to secure an aristocratic husband for her protégée.

Garrick and Violette never performed at the same theatre, but love blossomed at social gatherings, such as the Duke of Richmond's fireworks party, where Walpole noticed Garrick 'ogling and sighing the whole time' in her direction. Garrick's infatuation was widely reported in the gossip columns. Lady Burlington was eventually persuaded that Garrick would be a worthy husband, and her initial reservations were to become a matter of jest between them. Garrick wrote to Lady Burlington during his honeymoon, telling her that his new wife 'has more than once confessed to me that though she liked me very well, and was determined not to marry anybody else, yet she was as determined not to marry me if Your Ladyship had put a negative upon me'. The Garricks spent part of their honeymoon at the Burlingtons' villa at Chiswick, and Eva Maria was generously remembered in Lady Burlington's will. Garrick remained an adoring husband, and described his wife in verse:

4. Georg Christoph Lichtenberg, *Lichtenberg's Visits to England*, Oxford 1938, pp. 9–10.

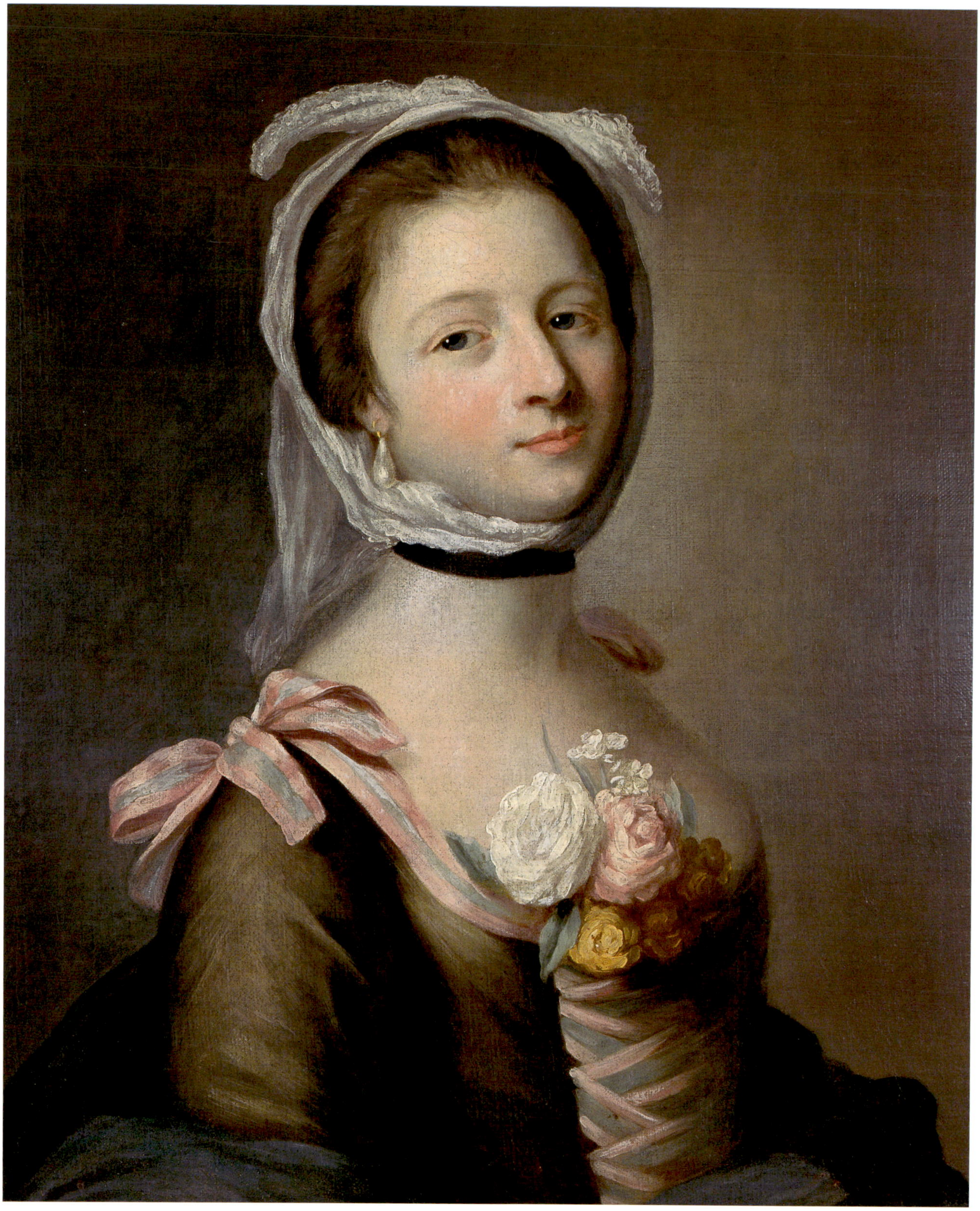

9 Katherine Read, *Eva Maria Garrick*
Private Collection.

A gaiety with innocence,
A soft address, with manly sense,
Ravishing manners, void of art,
A cheerful, firm, yet feeling heart,
Beauty, that charms all public gaze,
And humble, amid pomp and praise...

Katherine Read was highly regarded as a portraitist, particularly for her work in pastel. She had contact with the theatre, making portraits of the actresses Susanna Cibber and Peg Woffington.[5] She made another similar portrait of Mrs Garrick, in pastel (Victoria & Albert Museum), and Garrick may have sat to her also.[6] Many years later, Fanny Burney wrote a poignant description of Read in her journal:

> a very clever woman, & in her Profession has certainly very great merit; but her turn of mind is naturally melancholy, she is Absent, full of Care, & has a Countenance the most haggard & wretched I ever saw, added to which she Dresses in a style most strange & Queer that can be conceived, &, Which is worst of all, is always very Dirty.[7] RB

10 **Louis François Roubiliac (1702–1762)**
David Garrick, 1758
Gilt Bronze, 25 × 21 cm
The Garrick Club
INSCRIBED *DAVID GARRICK.* Arm, / *L.F. Roubiliac Sct. ad Vivum* / 1758

This bust was made the year Roubiliac completed Garrick's commission for a life-size statue of Shakespeare, intended for his Shakespeare Temple in the grounds of the villa at Hampton. The statue can be glimpsed through the door in Zoffany's portrait of Garrick and his wife on the steps of the Temple in 1762 (cat. no. 16). Garrick bequeathed the statue to the British Museum. In the same year Roubiliac also made a terracotta bust of Garrick, now lost (plaster cast in the National Portrait Gallery), which compares to this bronze bust. The artist Adrien Carpentiers painted Roubiliac working on the maquette of the Shakespeare statue (National Portrait Gallery) and Andrea Soldi painted Roubiliac working on this terracotta bust of Garrick (Garrick Club) in 1757. Both portraits were engraved, enhancing the fame of the sculptor by his association with Garrick. There were four plaster medallions, three wax medallions and two terracotta busts of Garrick in Roubiliac's sale, after his death in 1762.

Roubiliac frequented Slaughter's Coffee House, becoming part of the literary and artistic circle which met there, including William Hogarth. He may have gained an introduction to Garrick through this group. Roubiliac achieved fame in London in 1738 with his statue of George Frideric Handel, commissioned for the pleasure gardens at Vauxhall (Victoria & Albert Museum), which may have inspired Garrick to commission Roubiliac to create a statue of Shakespeare. RB

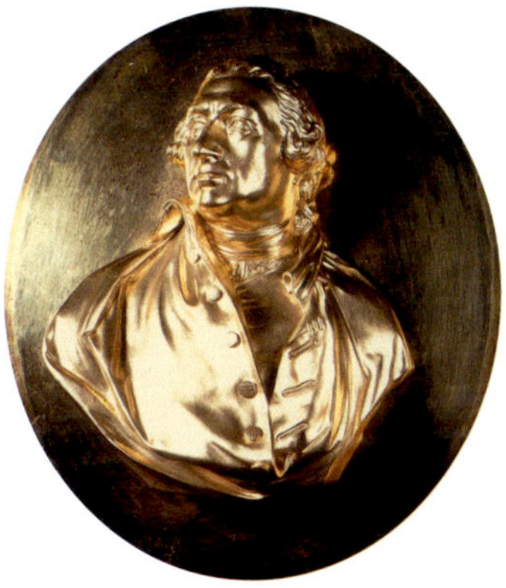

10 **Louis François Roubiliac**
Bust of David Garrick
Photograph courtesy of The Art Archive/ Garrick Club.

5. Margery Morgan, 'Katherine Read: A Woman Painter in Romney's London', *Transactions of the Romney Society*, IV, 1999, pp. 12–17.

6. Percy Fitzgerald, *Life of Garrick*, London 1899, p. 101.

7. Lars E. Troide (ed.), *The Early Journals and Letters of Fanny Burney*, 2 vols., Oxford 1990, II, p. 70.

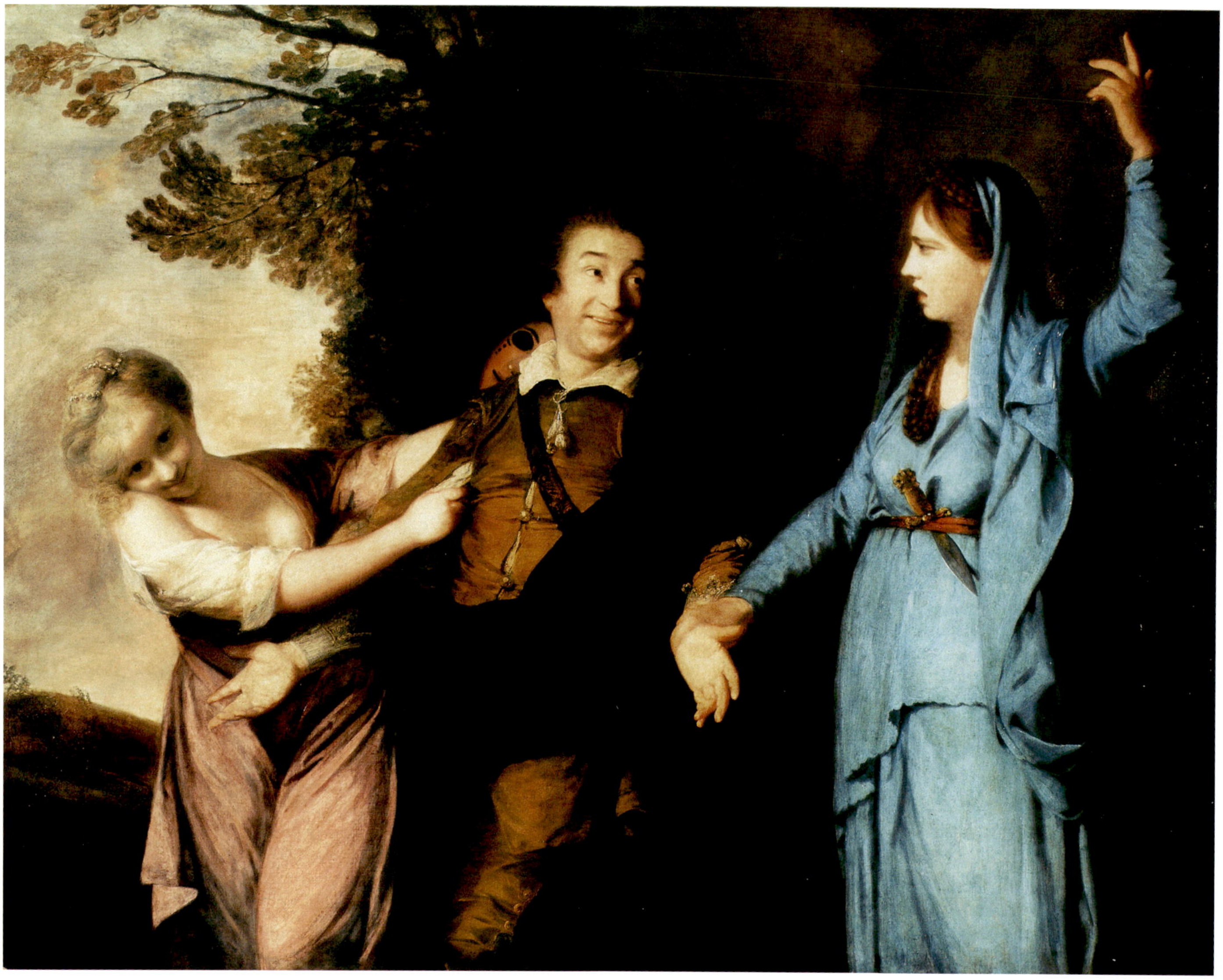

11 Sir Joshua Reynolds
David Garrick between Tragedy and Comedy
Waddesdon, The Rothschild Collection (Rothschild Family Trust / Mike Fear).

11 Sir Joshua Reynolds (1723–1792)
David Garrick between Tragedy and Comedy, *1761*
Oil on canvas, 148 × 183 cm
Waddesdon, The Rothschild Collection (Rothschild Family Trust)

This painting was purchased from Reynolds by George Montagu-Dunk, 2nd Earl of Halifax, for about 300 guineas. He was probably advised on the purchase by his secretary at the time, the playwright Richard Cumberland. Cumberland wrote an epilogue to his comedy *The Brothers*, which ran at Covent Garden in 1769, deliberately flattering Garrick and Reynolds:

> Who but has seen the celebrated strife,
> Where Reynolds calls the canvas into life,
> And 'twixt the Tragic and the Comic muse,
> Courted of both, and dubious where to choose,
> Th'immortal Actor stands?

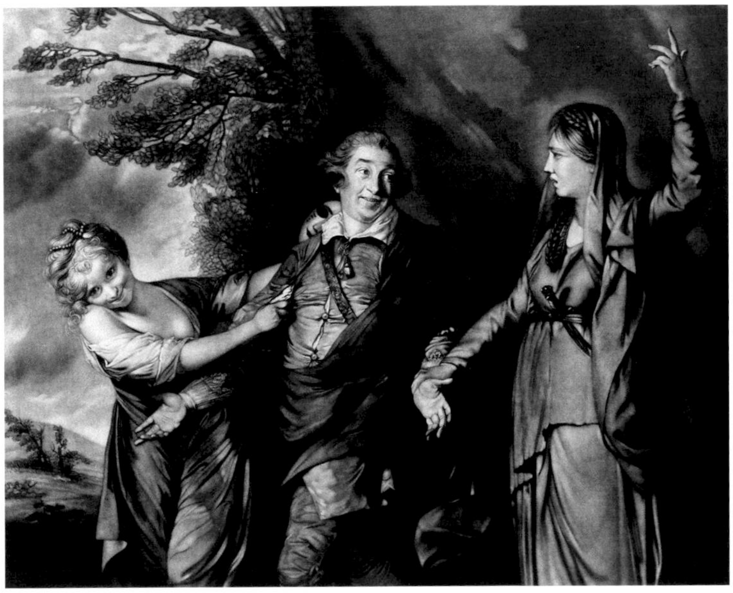

12 **Edward Fisher**
after Sir Joshua Reynolds
Mr. Garrick between Tragedy and Comedy
Lennox-Boyd Collection.

Garrick was impressed, and produced Cumberland's *The West Indian* at Drury Lane in 1771. It proved to be the outstanding success of the year. Cumberland introduced Garrick to another fashionable portrait painter, George Romney. Although Garrick sat to Romney in the 1770s, it seems that no finished portrait was produced. Despite Cumberland's admiration for Reynolds's work, he was not particularly fond of the man himself. In a conversation between Garrick and Reynolds, recorded by Northcote, Garrick attempts to offer Reynolds an explanation for Cumberland's dislike:

> He hates you, Sir Joshua, because you do not admire the painter whom he considers as a second Corregio'. 'Who is that?' replied Sir Joshua. 'Why, his Corregio,' answered Garrick, 'is Romney the painter!'.[8]

RB

12 Edward Fisher (1730–1781) after Sir Joshua Reynolds (1723–1792)

***Mr. Garrick between Tragedy and Comedy**, 1762*
Mezzotint engraving, 40.2 × 50.2 cm
Lennox-Boyd Collection
Proof before letters

This mezzotint was exhibited with Reynolds's painting at the Society of Artists exhibition in 1762. It is the first print that Garrick requests in his letter to his brother from Paris in 1764 (see p.13), and it appears that Garrick and Fisher had done business before:

> You may apply to ye Engraver he lives in Leicester Fields, & his name is Fisher, he will give you good ones, if he knows they are for Me

When Cumberland praised Reynolds's picture in the epilogue to his play *The Brothers* (see cat. no. 11) in 1769, the audience were able to understand this reference because of the popularity

8. James Northcote, *Memoirs of Sir Joshua Reynolds*, 2nd edition, 2 Vols., London 1819, I, p. 234.

of engraved versions of the picture. When Garrick's friend and collaborator George Colman visited Paris in 1765, he reported to Garrick, with reference to the print by J.E Haid, that:

> There hang out here in every street, pirated prints of Reynolds's Picture of you, which are underwritten, 'L'homme entre le Vice et la Virtu'.

RB

13 James McArdell (*c.*1728–1765) after Benjamin Wilson (1721–1788)

***David Garrick as King Lear with Kent and the Fool in a Storm**, 1761*
Mezzotint Engraving, 38 × 50.6 cm
Trustees of the British Museum
INSCRIBED *B:Wilson Pinx.^{t} ***J.^{s} Mc Ardell fecit.* / Mr Garrick *in the* Character *of* King Lear. / *Act 3.^{d} Scene 1.st / Done from ye Original Picture in the Collection of Henry Hoare Esqr – ***Publish'd accord.g to Act of Parliament;* 1761. *& sold at the Golden Head in Cov^{t} G.*

In this scene, Garrick, as Lear, has been turned out onto the heath during a storm by his daughters Goneril and Regan. He is beginning to lose his mind. Lear is accompanied by Edgar in disguise as 'Poor Tom', played by William Havard, and also Kent, probably played by Astley Brandsby. Thomas Wilkes describes the affecting performance:

> I never see him coming down from one corner of the Stage, with his old grey hair standing, as it were, erect upon his head, his face filled with horror and attention, his hands expanded and his whole frame actuated by a dreadful solemnity, but I am astounded and share in all his distress.[9]

It was said that Garrick had managed to convey a most convincing madness by observing a friend who had lost his senses after a tragic accident, in which he had allowed his small daughter to fall from an open window.[10]

Garrick first appeared as Lear in spring of 1742, at the Goodman's Fields Theatre, in Nahum Tate's 1681 version of the play *The True and Ancient History of King Lear and His Three Daughters*, which eliminated the character of the Fool, made Cordelia enamoured of Edgar and gave the play a happy ending, where Lear's lost kingdom is returned to him. In 1756 Garrick restored much of Shakespeare's original dialogue to the play, but did not reinstate the original ending, or the character of the Fool, who was considered too distracting.

During the 1756–7 season, Garrick and Spranger Barry were competing as rival Lears, and Wilson may have painted this scene to commemorate Garrick's acknowledged triumph. McArdell's engraving after this painting is the first large-scale, landscape-format mezzotint of a theatrical scene. It was one of the prints Garrick requested his brother send to him in Paris in 1764. Wilson has depicted this scene from Lear in much the same way as Garrick had described it to Hayman in 1745 (cat. no. 7), although Garrick includes the Fool for a more literal representation. It is possible that Garrick's ideas on how to represent this scene visually had not altered since then, and that he was making similar suggestions to Wilson. The original painting is now lost.

RB

9. Thomas Wilkes, *A General View of the Stage*, 1759, p. 234.

10. Ian McIntyre, *Garrick*, London 1999, p. 49.

14 Johan Zoffany (1733–1810)

David Garrick in 'The Farmer's Return', 1762

Oil on Canvas, 101.6 × 127 cm

Lambton Trustees

(Illustrated on p.20)

The plot of this short comedy exploited the feverish interest in the 'Cock Lane Ghost', a supernatural phenomenon that focused the public's attention on a small house in Smithfield, London. The house was believed to be haunted by the ghost of Fanny Lynes, who conveyed messages by a series of knocks and scratches, through the medium of a twelve-year-old girl. It was eventually exposed as a hoax.

The Farmer's Return is only ninety-four lines long and was written by Garrick as an 'Interlude' during a benefit evening for the actress Mrs Pritchard (see cat. no. 30). Garrick took the role of the farmer, newly returned from London, where he had witnessed many wondrous sights, including the coronation procession of George III and a play. He also made the required pilgrimage to Cock Lane. On his return, he teased his devoted wife, played by Mrs Bradshaw, that the ghost had doubted her fidelity:

FARMER With her nails, and her knuckles, she answer'd so noice.
For *Yes* she knock'd *Once*, and for *No* she knocked *Twoice*.
I asked her *one* thing –
WIFE What thing?
FARMER If yo', Dame, was true?
WIFE And the poor soul knocked *one*.
FARMER By the zounds, it was *two*!
WIFE I'll not be abused, Jahn. (cries)
FARMER Come, prithee, no croying,
The ghoast, among friends, was much giv'n to loying.

This painting was Garrick's first commission from the German artist Zoffany, who had arrived in London the previous year. Zoffany completed the work in the two months between Garrick's first performance and the Society of Artists exhibition. It was his first major success in England. A contemporary newspaper critic wrote that the painting was:

> a most accurate representation on canvas of that scene as performed at Drury Lane. The painter absolutely transports us in imagination back again to the theatre.[11]

It is likely that Zoffany elaborated on the stage set when recreating the scene for this picture, creating a large room with greater depth and detail, emulating Dutch genre pictures. Hogarth had recorded the scene as a sketch, and the print after this drawing (cat. no. 15) shows a much simpler room than Zoffany's. The detail of the actual acting space probably lies somewhere between these two representations. Garrick hung this painting in the dining room of the Adelphi, opposite the fireplace. Zoffany painted a companion for this painting showing Garrick in *Venice Preserv'd* (cat. no. 19) later in the same year. RB

11. Quoted in Mary Webster, *Johan Zoffany* 1733–1810, (exhibition catalogue, National Portrait Gallery), London 1976, no. 10, p. 25.

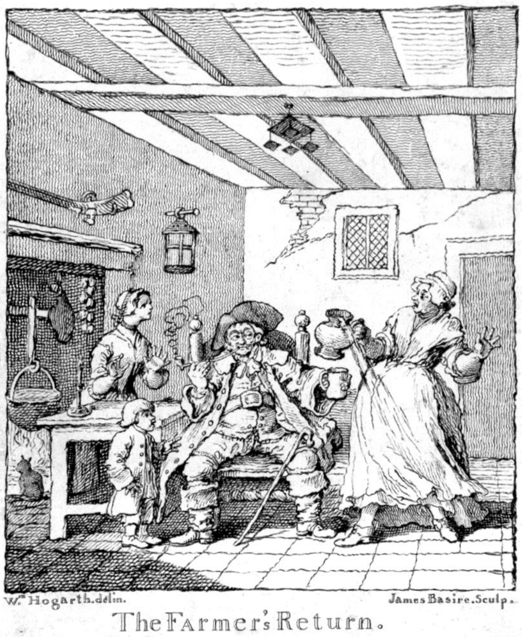

15 **James Basire after William Hogarth**
The Farmer's Return
Trustees of the British Museum.

15 James Basire (1730–1802) after William Hogarth (1697–1764)

The Farmer's Return, 1762
Engraving, 18 × 15.5 cm
Trustees of the British Museum
INSCRIBED *Wm. Hogarth. delin.James Basire. Sculp. / The Farmer's Return.*

This print was the frontispiece to the published version of Garrick's short play *The Farmer's Return*. It was accompanied by this dedication:

> The following Interlude was prepared for the Stage, merely with a View of assisting *Mrs. Pritchard* at her Benefit.... Notwithstanding the favourable Reception it has met with, the Author would not have printed it, had not his Friend, Mr. *Hogarth*, flattered him most agreeably, by thinking *The Farmer and his Family* not unworthy of a Sketch of his Pencil. To Him, therefore, this Trifle, which he has so much honoured, is inscribed, as a faint Testimony of the Sincere Esteem which the Writer bears him, both as a *Man* and an *Artist.*

Hogarth's original drawing, now lost, from which this print was taken, probably hung in Garrick's house in Southampton Street until the Garricks moved to the Adelphi terrace, where it hung in the green drawing room. Garrick's dedication implies that Hogarth's drawing was the first representation of this play. Hogarth did not make a painting from his drawing, but Garrick's obvious delight in the picture possibly inspired him to commission Zoffany to paint *The Farmer's Return* soon after, in time to be exhibited at the Society of Artists (cat. no. 14). Hogarth's drawing was known before the exhibition of Zoffany's painting, when Walpole cast his opinion: 'Good, like the actors, and the whole better than Hogarth's'.

Hogarth and Zoffany have depicted the same moment: the Farmer's children have just entered with a candle, pipe and some ale for their father, but the artists have represented the

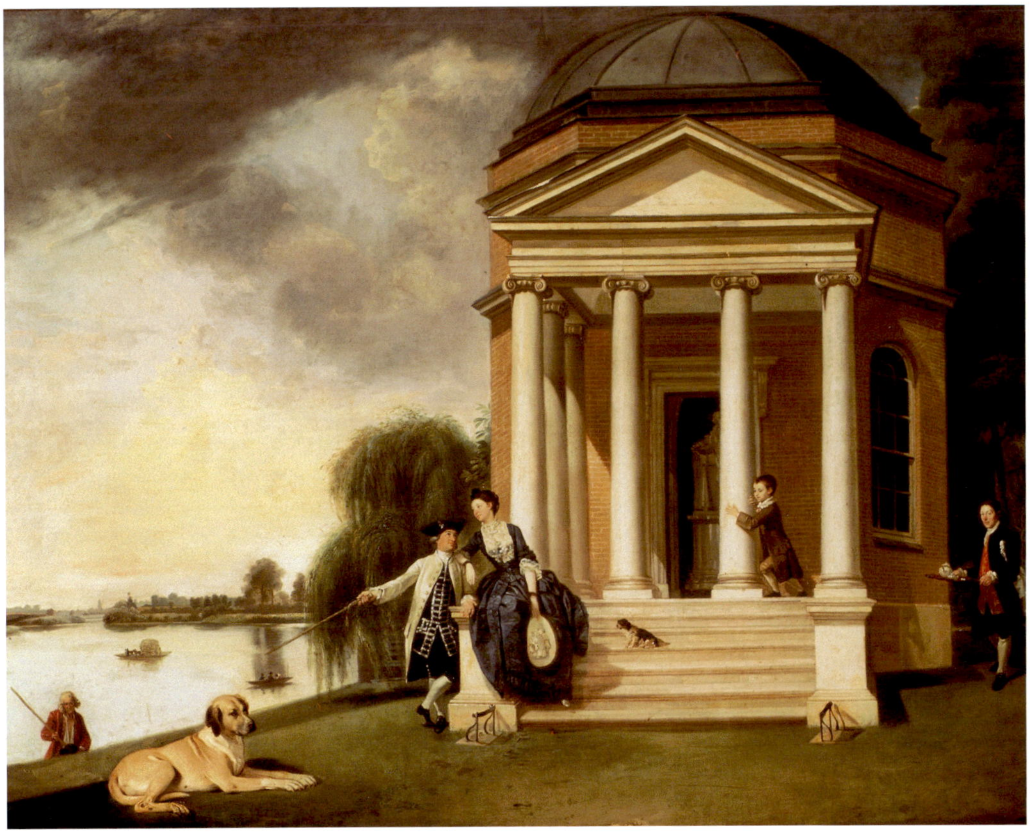

16 Johan Zoffany
Mrs and Mrs Garrick by the Shakespeare Temple at Hampton
Lambton Trustees.

acting space very differently. Basire's print shows that Hogarth drew a simple, rustic, room. The actual set was unlikely to have been very elaborate for so brief an 'interlude'. Hogarth may have simplified the back wall, including fewer objects than were actually present, for speed and ease when sketching. Both artists have included beamed ceilings, presumably not part of the set, in order to create the sense of a real interior. Basire's print shows that Hogarth did not paint specific portraits, but rather comical caricatures. Garrick, as the farmer, is wearing an old-fashioned jacket, and looks slightly more boorish than the gentleman farmer depicted by Zoffany. RB

16 Johan Zoffany (1733–1810)

Mrs and Mrs Garrick by the Shakespeare Temple at Hampton, 1762
Oil on canvas, 99.7 × 125 cm
Lambton Trustees

Mr and Mrs Garrick are shown leaning on the balustrade of the Shakespeare Temple at Hampton. The child on the steps is thought to be Garrick's nephew Carrington Garrick (1753–1787), eldest son of his brother George. The enormous dog is the Garricks' mastiff, Dragon.

Garrick met the artist in the studio of Benjamin Wilson, who was employing Zoffany as a painter of drapery. Wilson was a friend of the actor, and had painted Garrick in character, including *King Lear* (cat. no. 13). Garrick appears to have recognised Zoffany's talents as a painter immediately, and his first commission was the painting *The Farmer's Return* in 1762

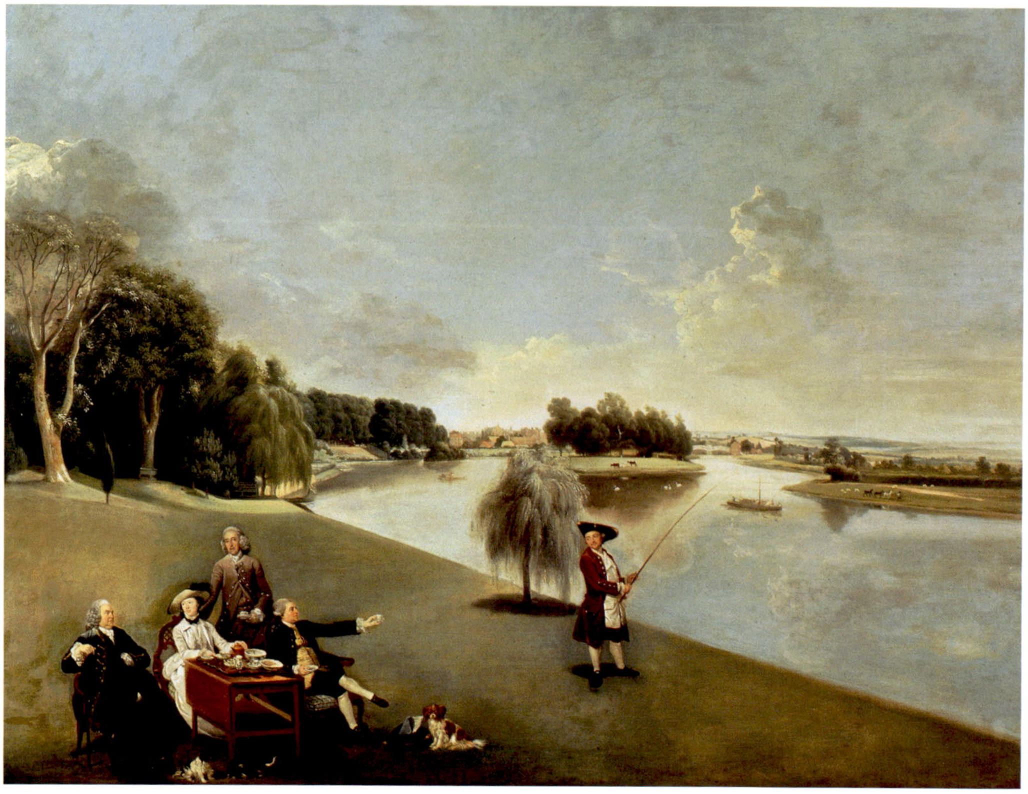

17 Johan Zoffany
A View in Hampton Garden with Mr and Mrs Garrick taking tea
Lambton Trustees.

(cat. no. 14). After the success of this painting, Garrick invited Zoffany to stay at Hampton in the summer of 1762, where Zoffany produced two conversation pieces and two smaller works showing the Garricks, their family and friends, enjoying the grounds of their riverside villa.

Garrick was affording Zoffany the sort of sustained patronage and level of intimacy that he had never previously offered an artist. Zoffany's stay would also, no doubt, have allowed Mrs Garrick a welcome opportunity to discourse in her mother tongue: Garrick often affectionately mimicked her strong accent, which she never lost. Wilson was understandably affronted by this show of favour and was, according to Garrick, 'Complaining in the streets'. In an unusually forthright tone, Garrick wrote to Wilson from Hampton, during Zoffany's stay, addressing the letter to an imagined intermediary called 'Mr Telltruth'. He suggests that Wilson; 'need not Employ his out runners and Spies to discover what Zoffani is doing at my house' and goes on to explain:

> I shall do his German friend all ye offices in my Power; he was warmly recommended to me by my Acquaintance, is a man of Merit, and well behaved in my family…he will be now at Liberty to begin the Conversation Piece he mentions, I rely on his fancy to make it *a most Exelent Picture.*

Garrick hung this portrait and its companion (cat. no. 17), in the dining room of the Adelphi, opposite Zoffany's paintings of Garrick in theatrical scenes (cat. no.s 19 and 14). Garrick and Wilson were eventually reconciled. In 1768, Garrick commissioned Wilson to paint a portrait of Shakespeare, as a gift to the Corporation of Stratford (destroyed by fire in 1946), and closely involved Wilson in preparations for the Shakespeare Jubilee of 1769. RB

17 Johan Zoffany (1733–1810)

A View in Hampton Garden with Mr and Mrs Garrick taking tea, 1762

Oil on canvas, 99.7 × 125 cm

Lambton Trustees

Garrick is seated on the right, and offers tea to his brother George, who is fishing. Mrs Garrick is pouring tea, while the Garricks' butler Charles Hart waits in attendance. The man seated to the left has been identified as George Bodens, described by Mrs Thrale as a man 'of much wit, Archness and a peculiar Vein of humour – his sayings are circulated about the Town'. Zoffany has taken this view of the garden from the steps of the Shakespeare Temple. RB

18 Johan Zoffany (1733–1810)

A View of Hampton House and Garden with Garrick writing, 1762

Oil on canvas, 61 × 73.6 cm

Petworth Collection

Garrick is sitting on the lawn, to the side of the villa at Hampton. A gardener is leading a horse pulling a lawn-roller. This scene, one of the set of paintings that Zoffany painted at Hampton during the summer of 1762, hung as an overdoor in the dining room of the Adelphi (see cat. no. 50). Zoffany created another overdoor for this room, completing the set of Hampton pictures, which is described in Garrick's inventory as 'View in the Garden and two Miss Garrick's at Play, whole length', but is now lost. Garrick appears to be enjoying a rare moment of repose here, but is probably working on a manuscript or adaptation. RB

19 Johan Zoffany (1733–1810)

David Garrick and Mrs Cibber as Jaffier and Belvidera in Thomas Otway's 'Venice Preserv'd', 1762

Oil on canvas, 101 × 127 cm

Lambton Trustees

This painting commemorates Garrick's last performance as Jaffier in *Venice Preserv'd*, a role he had played twenty times, in the autumn of 1762. Garrick originally took the lead role of Pierre, but from 1748, he preferred to play Pierre's friend Jaffier, a part that offered a greater range of passions and conflicting affections. Zoffany has depicted a moment of extreme dramatic tension: Jaffier feels his honour is impelling him to kill his wife Belvidera, whom he believes to have betrayed his friend Pierre. She faces him bravely:

Then be the next my doom.
I see thou'st pass'd my sentence in thy heart,
And I'll no longer weep or plead against it,
But with the humblest, most obedient patience
Meet thy dear hands, and kiss 'em when they wound me …

Belvidera's words touch Jaffier and he spares his wife, but resolves take his own life instead. It is the beginning of a tragic and gruesome climax which ends with the death of all three principals. Thomas Otway wrote *Venice Preserv'd* in 1681, and it became one of the most

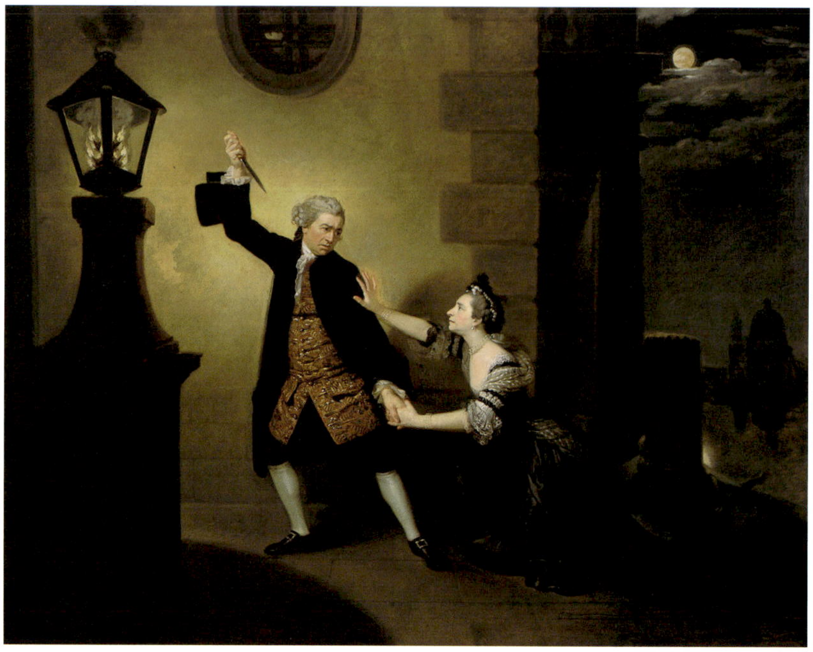

19 **Johan Zoffany**
David Garrick in 'Venice Preserv'd'
Lambton Trustees.

important and famous plays in the repertoire, regularly performed until the middle of the nineteenth century.

Garrick commissioned this painting and hung it in the dining room at his house in the Adelphi, as a pendant to Zoffany's portrait of Garrick in *The Farmer's Return* (cat. no. 14), painted earlier in the year, as a demonstration to his dinner quests that his talents were equal to both tragedy and comedy.

Zoffany's paintings of Garrick were very popular in reproduction (cat. no.s 20 and 30 and fig. 9), and his work for Garrick brought Zoffany to the attention of Queen Charlotte, for whom he painted many portraits of the royal family. RB

20 James McArdell (*c.* 1728–1765) after Johan Zoffany (1733–1810)
David Garrick with Mrs Cibber as Jaffier and Belvidera in Otway's 'Venice Preserv'd'*, 1764*
Mezzotint Engraving, 42.5 x 54.4 cm
Trustees of the British Museum
INSCRIBED *Zoffanij Pinx.*t***Ja.s M.cArdell fecit.* / M.r Garrick *and* M.rs Cibber *in the* Characters *of* Jaffier *and* Belvidera. / Venice Preserved *act* 4. *Scene* 2.d / *Publish'd March* 25. 1764. *according to Act of Parliament*****Sold by J. M.cArdell, at the Corner of Henrietta Street in Covent Garden.*

This was the first theatrical print to be made after a painting by Zoffany. An advertisement for it appeared in *The Public Advertiser* in January 1763:

Subscriptions to be taken in at Mr. Zaffanij's, in the Great Piazza, Covent Garden, and the Original Picture to be seen there till the Middle of February.[12]

12. Christopher Lennox-Boyd, G. Shaw, S. Halliwell, *Theatre: in the Age of Garrick. English mezzotints from the collection of the Hon. Christopher Lennox-Boyd* (exhibition catalogue, Courtauld Institute Galleries), London 1994, p. 56.

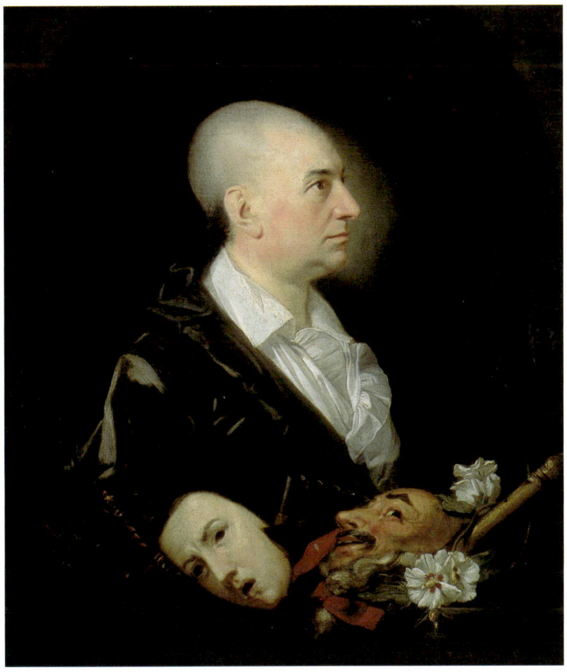

21 Johan Zoffany
David Garrick
The Ashmolean Museum, Oxford.

Zoffany was exhibiting his newly completed painting (cat. no. 19) at his studio in order to stimulate interest in the print, and also in his work in general. The fame of Garrick in the role of Jaffier, and the success of Zoffany's portrait of Garrick in *The Farmer's Return* at the Society of Artists exhibition the previous year, meant that this print was ensured success. The original painting was commissioned by Garrick and was exhibited at the Society of Artists during 1763, before being hung in his dining room at the Adelphi. This is one of the prints which Garrick requested his brother George send him in Paris, suggesting, as the advertisement states, that he obtain them from Zoffany himself. RB

21 Johan Zoffany (1733–1810)

David Garrick

Oil on canvas, 75.2 × 62.7 cm

The Ashmolean Museum, Oxford. Accepted by H.M. Government in lieu of Inheritance Tax and allocated to the Ashmolean Museum, 1999; WA 1999.10

In a receipt (in Italian) dated 23 April 1763, Zoffany acknowledged payment from Garrick for 'four views of the garden with portraits, a portrait in profile, one of Mrs Garrick and a portrait of Mr Colman, the Farmer's Return, Jaffier and Belvidera, and two frames'. Although the existence of the 'portrait in profile' has long been known from copies and prints, the recent acquisition by the Ashmolean of the prime version commissioned by Garrick has brought to light one of Zoffany's most sophisticated and complex masterpieces.

During the early nineteenth century, this painting (or another version) was known as the 'Colman Portrait', and was owned by Thomas Harris, the manager of Covent Garden, who also owned the portrait of Colman mentioned in the receipt above. When he sold the portrait in 1819, the catalogue entry purported to explain the circumstances of the commission:

> This picture is highly valued for the correctness of the likeness: it was painted for George Colman the elder. To avoid the different changes of countenance, with which Garrick used to amuse himself, while sitting for his portrait, Zoffany, took this likeness concealed in an anti-chamber, during the times of Garrick's shaving his head, 'his constant custom in the afternoon'.

It is more probable, however, that, as with the allegorical portrait by Reynolds (cat. no. 11), it was Garrick who suggested the general idea, if not the specific details. The informality of the sitter's dress, the head shaved except for the back hair left to hold the wig in place, must certainly have been Garrick's idea. The features are very closely observed, the loose skin around the eyes and chin frankly depicted, the whole effect truthful rather than flattering.

As Edgar Wind has shown in his brilliant exegesis of the Reynolds, the depiction of an actor equally affecting in both tragedy and comedy was based on Garrick's own belief that one can only be a good tragedian by being a good comic actor. Wind has further shown that the inclusion of Melpomene and Thalia, the muses of Tragedy and Comedy, was an obvious device, suggested by their presence as statues on the stage, and one which was frequently adopted in engravings of actors. As a close associate of Garrick, Zoffany was no doubt aware of his theories of acting, and would have known of precedents for his composition in continental engravings. Zoffany has modified the iconography slightly, for, while the mask of Tragedy is a distraught female, as one would expect, that of Comedy is in fact the living face of a leering satyr. The other attributes of Tragedy are a dagger, sprigs of cypress associated with death, and ivy, symbolising immortality; while with Comedy are flowers, pan pipes and a recorder, instruments associated with satyrs, and a branch of bay laurel, generally an attribute of a literary or artistic sitter.

CH

22 Johan Zoffany (1733–1810)
David Garrick in Sir John Vanbrugh's 'The Provok'd Wife', 1763-65
Oil on canvas, 99 × 124.5 cm
Wolverhampton Art Gallery
(Illustrated on p. 16)

Zoffany has depicted Act IV scene I of Sir John Vanbrugh's comedy *The Provok'd Wife,* as it was performed on 18 April 1763. The actors playing the watchmen can be identified as Henry Vaughan, Hullet, Thomas Clough, William Parsons, Thomas Phillips and Watkins, some of the 'stable' of actors that Garrick created at Drury Lane. Garrick, as Sir John Brute, has spent a drunken evening with his friends Lord Rake and Colonel Bully. He is wearing a set of clothes stolen from a journeyman tailor, which were intended for his own wife. He is resisting arrest by the watch, exclaiming that he is, in fact, Queen Boudicca:

> Sirrah, I am Bonduca, Queen of the Welchmen; and with a leek as long as my pedigree, I will destroy your Roman legions in an instant. Britons, Strike home.

Vanbrugh's original play, written in 1697, included sexual references which had shocked audiences. Garrick reworked the play, excluding any offensive language, and also making the plot more concise. The role of Sir John Brute was a challenge indeed, since audiences identified the part with Garrick's rival James Quin, who had played Sir John since 1719. Garrick, of course, attempted a new interpretation of the role. A contemporary commentator, Christoph Lichtenberg, compared the two: 'Some theatregoers preferred Quin's coarse drunk-sodden boor: but a great number were taken by Garrick's gentleman debauchee'.[13] Henry Angelo notes that Zoffany began this painting at his studio in Covent Garden:

> he also took his first studies from Garrick, for the drunken scene in the *Provok'd Wife* here; and my father (Domenico Angelo, the fencing master and stage designer) accompanied him thither from his house in Southampton Street, adjacent, and Fosbrook brought the dress from the theatre, for Garrick to put on, to be painted in. This picture was not finished, however, until Zoffany had removed to Lincoln's Inn Fields.[14]

This description affords us insight into Zoffany's approach to painting theatrical scenes. He invited actors in costume to sit for him at his studio, but his sketches of Garrick as Abel Drugger (cat. no. 36) suggest that he also made preliminary sketches of the actors at the theatre, during rehearsal. This painting was exhibited at the Society of Artists in 1765. A painting of *Mr Garrick as Sir John Brute* by Zoffany hung in the dining room at Hampton. It is described in more detail in the sale catalogue for the contents of the Hampton villa after Mrs Garrick's death in 1823: *A small whole length portrait of Mr Garrick in the character of Sir John Brute*. It seems, therefore, that it is the figure study of Garrick as Sir John (Maugham Collection, National Theatre), in which the head is said to have been altered at Garrick's request, that hung in the dining room at Hampton. This larger painting is not listed in Garrick's inventories. RB

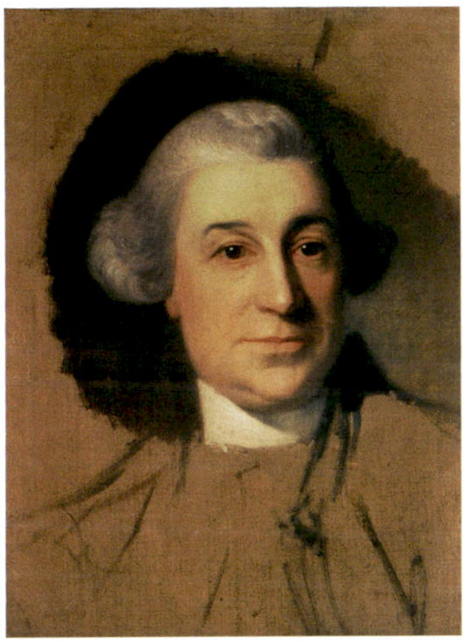

23 **Johan Zoffany,**
Portrait of David Garrick
The Art Archive the Garrick Club .

23 Johan Zoffany (1733-1810)

David Garrick
Oil on canvas, 47 × 35 cm
The Garrick Club

As well as theatrical scenes and conversation pieces, Zoffany painted two single-figure portraits of Garrick: a classicising profile (cat. no. 21), and this unfinished work. It is not certain why Zoffany did not complete this powerful likeness. The canvas has been cut down, indicating that this head was intended as part of a larger work.

Like Hogarth and Gainsborough, Zoffany experienced difficulty painting Garrick's head (see cat. no. 59). Garrick took James Boswell to Zoffany's studio in Covent Garden, a visit that Boswell recorded in his diary in January 1763. Garrick complained to Zoffany: 'you have made one of those heads for me *longer* than the other, and I would not willingly have it shortened'.[15] Zoffany also painted a portrait of Mrs Garrick with a mask, which was in the Hampton sale of 1823, but is untraced.

The first owner of the portrait was the actor Robert Baddeley (1732–94), who was himself painted in character by Zoffany. Baddeley had caused Garrick some headaches at Drury Lane because of the tempestuous relationship he shared with his wife, the actress Sophia Baddeley. Baddeley's ownership of this portrait testifies to his respect for Garrick as a colleague and manager. RB

13. Georg Christoph Lichtenberg, *Lichtenberg's Visits to England*, Oxford 1938, p. 71.

14. Shearer West, *The Image of the Actor*, London 1991, p. 64.

15. Frederick A. Pottle (ed.), *Boswell's London Journal* 1762-3, London, 1950, p. 141.

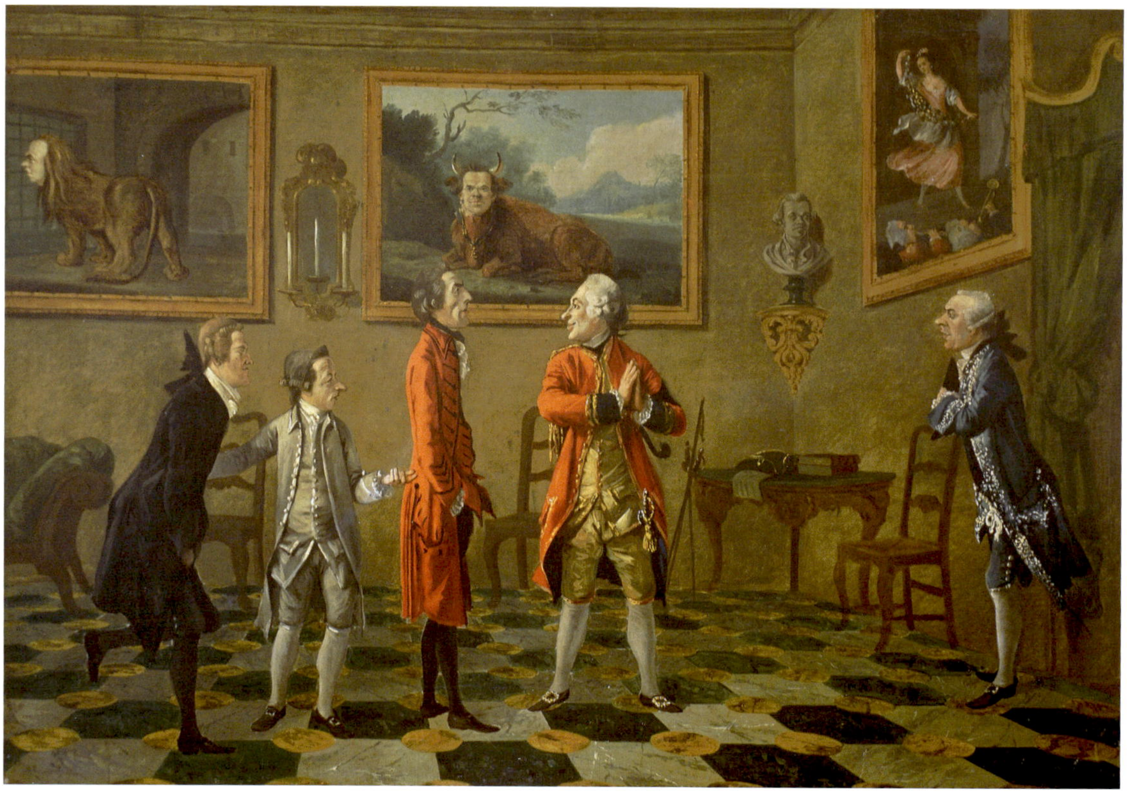

24 Thomas Patch
David Garrick in Italy
Exeter City Museums and Art Gallery.

24 Thomas Patch (1725–1782)

David Garrick in Italy, 1763
Oil on canvas, 102.1 × 136.3 cm
Exeter City Museums and Art Gallery

Garrick visited Florence in November 1763, as part of his continental tour. Patch shows him facing his three companions and enthusing over the picture of the dancer on the wall, an allusion to Garrick's wife Eva Maria (formerly a professional dancer), who was travelling with her husband. Garrick was conscious that his devotion to his wife, and his decision to travel with her, certainly distinguished him from his fellow British tourists. When Mrs Garrick suffered an attack of rheumatism in her hip, Garrick confided to the Duke of Devonshire:

> Tho some Husbands would hav rejoic'd to have their Wives tyd by ye leg; yet I must confess that I have been fool Enough to wish her Ev'n at ye top of Vesuvious with Me.

The figure on the far right of the picture is accepted to be Sir Horace Mann, who is also caricatured in the picture of the bull on the wall. Mann (1701–1786) was the British envoy at Florence, host to many British visitors there, and regular correspondent with Horace Walpole. The identity of the other figures is not known. Walpole wrote to Mann, telling him to expect:

> the famous Garrick and his once famous wife. He will make you laugh, as a mimic, and as he knows we are great friends, will affect great partiality for me; but be a little on your guard, remember he is *an actor*!

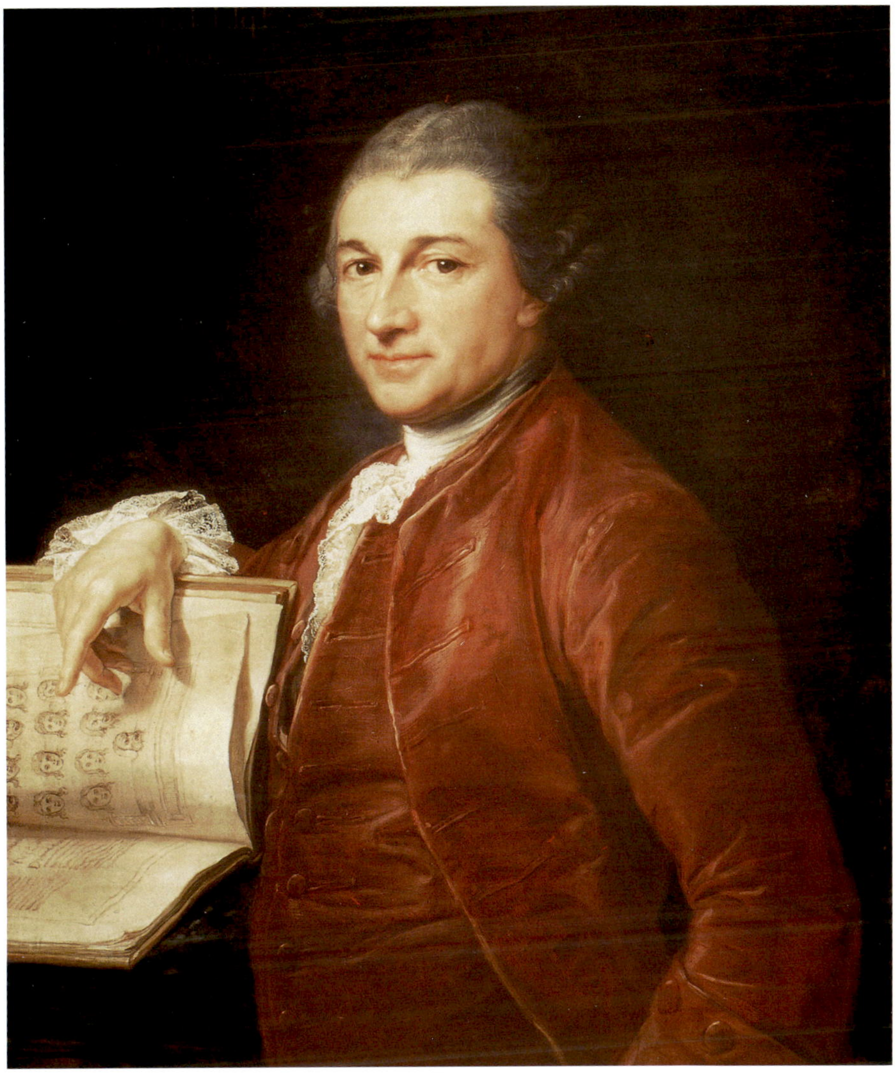

25 **Pompeo Batoni**
David Garrick
The Ashmolean Museum, Oxford.

Patch was the son of an Exeter doctor. He travelled to Italy, initially settling in Rome in 1747, and moved to Florence in 1755 where he gained introductions to English tourists through his friend Mann. He made his living painting landscape views and copies of Old Masters and began painting caricature groups of Grand Tourists and Anglo-Florentine society in the 1760s.

RB

25 Pompeo Batoni (1708–1787)

David Garrick, 1764

Oil on canvas, 76 × 63.5 cm

Ashmolean Museum, Oxford, Presented by Sir Richard Kaye, 1827

INSCRIBED (by a later hand at upper left) *David Garrick Esq. / given at Rome./* 1764.

Garrick was staying in Rome in December 1763 for a fortnight when he commissioned this portrait. He returned to Rome at the end of February, and sittings resumed. The painting was in Batoni's showroom by 6 May 1764.

A fascinating incident involving Garrick and a fellow tourist, discussed in a recent article by Catherine Whistler, reveals something of Garrick's attitude to his own portrait. Even before completion, Garrick had promised this portrait to the Reverend Richard Kaye, in exchange for a sardonyx cameo of a mask of a Bacchanal, purchased from a gardener at the Baths of Caracalla. According to Kaye 'the bargain was very politely struck on both sides'.[16] The Garricks met Kaye in Florence in 1763, where the unlucky Reverend was 'beat constantly by Mrs Garrick at Chess'. In 1765 Garrick borrowed the picture to have a copy made, perhaps regretting parting with the original: 'Your picture has not yet been out of my house, for the Copyer is so busy, he can't begin until the latter End of next week', although a copy does not appear in Garrick's later inventories.

Garrick is shown holding the 1736 Latin and Italian edition of Terence's *Comedies*, with illustrations by Giovanni Battista Sintes. He points to a page of masks for the comic drama *Andria*. Batoni was established as the portraitist of choice for wealthy English Grand Tourists, whom he depicted as cultivated, leisured gentlemen. This volume no doubt refers to Garrick's role as actor and playwright, and also as connoisseur and antiquarian. Garrick may have suggested the Terence himself as a nod to his friend George Colman who was working on an English translation of Terence's plays, and dedicated the *Phormio* to Garrick. Colman was also minding the Theatre Royal in Garrick's absence. The two were frequent correspondents during Garrick's Continental tour, and were collaborating to write the play *The Clandestine Marriage*. Garrick was working on drafts of this play whilst travelling. It could also be possible that Garrick suggested this particular page of the Terence after he had struck his deal with Kaye, an allusion to the subject matter of the prized cameo.

A few years earlier, Hogarth had painted the actor composing the prologue to Samuel Foote's play *Taste* (fig. 4), in which Garrick, as 'Peter Puff' the auctioneer, ridicules his customers, rich collectors who would pay inflated prices for any works of art painted by a so-called called 'Old Master', or called 'Classical' – sentiments which owed much to Hogarth's opinion of the British art market. It appears, however, that time in Italy, and the company of Grand Tourists, turned Garrick into a gentleman connoisseur. 'You must know I am antiquity-hunting from Morning to Night' he told George Colman from Rome. His new passion continued unabated in Padua, from where Garrick informed a fellow connoisseur, the Duke of Devonshire, that he was at that moment negotiating the purchase of 'no less than two Bassans, a Vandyke, a Rubens, a Paul Veronese &c', and he goes on to make light of his changed attitude: 'I don't see why I should not be a little ridiculous, as well as My betters'. RB

26 Angelica Kauffman (1741–1807)

David Garrick, 1764

Oil on canvas, 82 × 69 cm

The Burghley House Collection

INSCRIBED *Angelica Kauffman pinxt Ano 1764 at Naples*

Garrick sat to the Swiss artist Kauffman in Naples in early 1764. He was probably introduced to her by his new friend Nathaniel Dance, who was at the time engaged to Kauffman. She used the portrait to herald her arrival in England in 1765, when it was shown at the Free Society of Artists as *Portrait of a Gentleman*, 'From Miss Angelica Kaufman in Rome', and identified in one catalogue as representing Garrick. For Kauffman, Garrick wrote this short verse:

16. Catherine Whistler, 'The Exchange of gifts between David Garrick and Richard Kaye', *Burlington Magazine*, CXXXIX, No. 1130, May 1997, p. 329.

While thus you paint with ease and grace
And spirit all your own
Take if you please my mind and face
BUT LET MY HEART ALONE.[17]

The painting was soon acquired by Lord Exeter, with whom Garrick dined 'almost every day and night' in Naples. It is not certain whether the commission of this portrait was initiated by Garrick, Exeter or Kauffman. Exeter had just sat to Kauffman himself (sold Christies, 1982), and he bought several of her history pictures when he returned to England. If he initiated the commission, it signifies the esteem in which he held both his friend, and this newly emerging artist. Alternatively, Kauffman may have invited Garrick to sit for her, recognising that his celebrity could promote her own work. If the portrait was commissioned by Garrick himself, he probably gave it to Exeter as gift, a remembrance of time spent together in Naples.

In 1767, Garrick visited Kauffman at her house in Golden Square, where she had established a portrait practice, probably in order to see her portrait of Reynolds (Saltram, The National Trust). RB

27 Pietro Longhi (1700/02–1785)

Called Garrick delivering a scene from 'Macbeth' to the Duke of Parma, 1764
Oil on canvas, 48 × 61 cm
National Museums Liverpool (The Walker)

Garrick visited Parma in the spring of 1764. He was introduced to Philip, Duke of Parma (1720-1765) by the Duke of York, and described the evening in a letter to an unknown recipient, written from Padua. The Italian Duke had read Shakespeare, and was 'very desirous to hear our manner of speaking, which desire he shewed with so much feeling and delicacy, that I, readily consented, in presence of the duke of York, Lord Spencer, and the first minister.'

Arthur Murphy, an early biographer of Garrick who had been in the company at Drury Lane, elaborates on the occasion, identifying *Macbeth*, and in particular the dagger-scene, as the play from which Garrick performed extracts: 'His words were not understood, but his countenance expressed every sentiment, and every tone of the passions'.[18]

Longhi has depicted the masks of Tragedy and Comedy beneath Garrick's chair, and the winged figure of Fame has joined the elegant company to herald the actor's presence. It is not possible to identify accurately all the members of the select audience, although it has been suggested that the man at the right-hand end of the front row may be John, 1st Earl Spencer, and the man standing a little way behind him is perhaps Edward, Duke of York, acting as host for the evening.[19] According to Garrick, his recital made an extremely favourable impression on the Duke:

> He was greatly pleased, and the next morning sent me a very handsome gold box, with some of the finest enamelled painting upon all the sides of it I ever saw – He likewise ordered apartments for me, and sent me from his court more conceited by half than I came to it.

17. Percy Fitzgerald, *The Life of David Garrick,* London 1899, p. 326.

18. Arthur Murphy, *The Life of David Garrick, Esq.*, London 1801, p. 15.

19. Peter Walch, 'David Garrick in Italy', *Eighteenth-Century Studies*, Vol. 3, Issue 4 (Summer 1970), pp. 523–531.

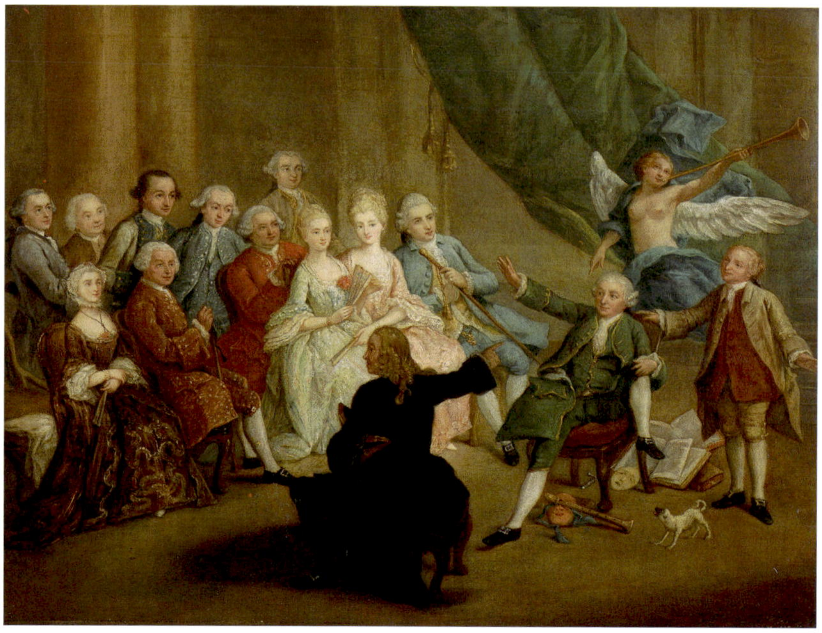

27 **Pietro Longhi**
Garrick delivering a scene from 'Macbeth'
National Museums Liverpool (The Walker).

Longhi was based in Venice, and it is not known whether he was actually present at this recital. Longhi's painting of interiors depicting noble life were extremely popular, and this portrait was perhaps commissioned by one of the English members of Garrick's audience who carried it to this country on his return.

Since then, the exact subject of the scene has become obscured. The painting was called *Garrick in the Green Room* when it was published as a mezzotint by George Daniel in 1829, and the audience was identified as some of the company of the Theatre Royal, Drury Lane, including Mr Woodward, Mr Macklin, Mrs Yates and Mrs Abington. It was attributed to Hogarth until 1933, when a drawing of the same scene, inscribed *Longhi*, was discovered in the Correr Museum in Venice, confirming that it had been painted in Italy. RB

28 Simon Francis Ravenet (1706 or 1721–1774) after Benjamin Wilson (1721–1788)

***David Garrick with Mrs Bellamy, as Romeo and Juliet, the scene in the monument**, 1765*

Mezzotint Engraving, 38.8 × 51.25 cm

Trustees of the British Museum

INSCRIBED *Mr Garrick and Miss Bellamy in the Characters of Romeo and Juliet / Designed and Painted by B. Wilson Engraved by R. S. Ravenet Published according to Act of Parlit by J. Boydell Engraver in Cheapside* 1765.

The moment depicted actually occurs during the seventy-five lines of text that Garrick added to *Romeo and Juliet*, which allowed Juliet to awake while Romeo was still alive, in order that they might share a final, tragic embrace. Garrick cast Spranger Barry and Mrs Cibber as the lovers in his revival of the play in 1748, and they enjoyed great success. However, when the play was not produced at Drury Lane the following year, the two principals defected to the theatre at Covent Garden, citing Garrick's jealousy of their success as their motive.

In the autumn of 1750, the two houses staged rival productions of *Romeo and Juliet*. At

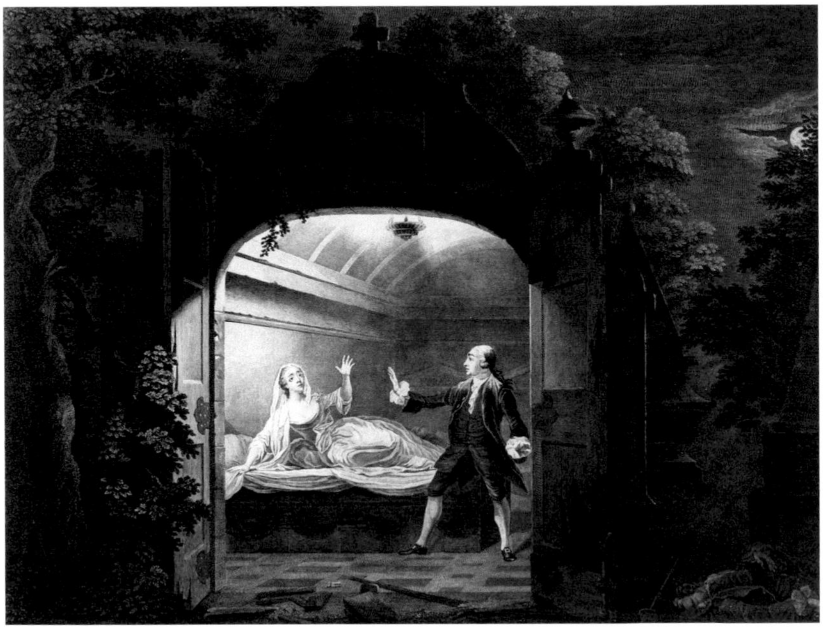

28 Simon Francis Ravenet
after Benjamin Wilson
David Garrick in 'Romeo and Juliet'
Trustees of the British Museum.

Drury Lane, Garrick took on the role of Romeo himself, and gave the young actress George Ann Bellamy intensive training for the role of Juliet. They performed for twelve nights in direct opposition, some members of the audience switching theatres mid-way through the performances. Barry's Romeo was tender and seductive, whereas Garrick's interpretation was passionate and fiery. Opinion remained divided; Garrick commanding 'most applause – Mr Barry most tears…'.[20]

RB

29 Sir Joshua Reynolds (1723–1792)

David Garrick as Kitely in 'Every Man in his Humour', 1767
Oil on canvas, 148 × 183 cm
The Royal Collection

When Garrick decided to revive Ben Jonson's play, *Every Man in his Humour*, written in 1598, it had not been performed since 1715. He worked on the text for over a year, before presenting it at Drury Lane in 1751, taking the role of Kitely, a merchant devoured by jealousy over his wife. Garrick was probably aware that the role had been played by Shakespeare in Jonson's original production. His adaptation was a great success and Garrick went on to play Kitely eighty times. Finlayson's mezzotint of Reynolds's portrait identifies it as showing Act II, scene 1, when Kitely resolves to be vigilant of his wife: 'Yea, every look or glance mine eye ejects/ Shall check occasion.'

However, it is unlikely that Reynolds had this particular moment in mind when he painted Garrick as Kitely, probably seeking to capture the character – the 'humour' – embodied by Garrick as Kitely, rather than a specific scene or moment. In his thirteenth discourse Reynolds writes: 'If a Painter should endeavour to copy the theatrical pomp and parade of dress and attitude, instead of that simplicity, which is not a greater beauty in life, than it is in Painting, we should condemn such Pictures as painted in the meanest style'. However, it seems Reynolds

20. Francis Gentleman, *The Dramatic Censor; or Critical Companion*, 2 Vols., London 1770, I, pp. 189–190.

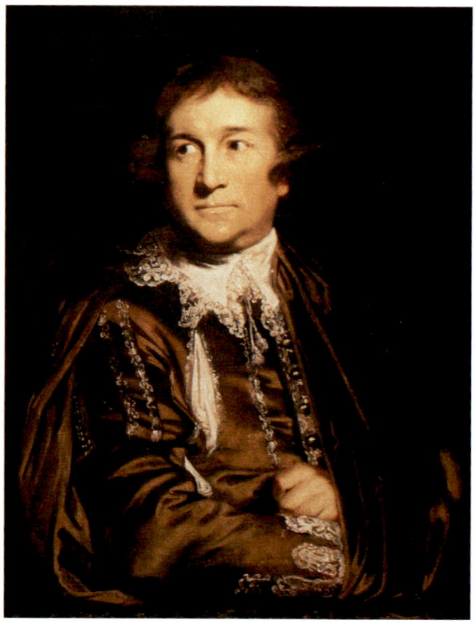

29 **Sir Joshua Reynolds**
David Garrick as Kitely in 'Every Man in his Humour'
The Royal Collection © 2003, Her Majesty Queen Elizabeth II.

was an admirer of Zoffany's paintings of Garrick in character, purchasing Zoffany's *Garrick as Abel Drugger in The Alchymist* (see. cat. no. 36 and fig. 9).

In 1772, Northcote reported that Reynolds also intended to paint a multiple portrait of Garrick 'in a great many different characters':

> he is to be in his proper character in the middle, speaking a prologue, and about fifteen of the most remarkable characters which he has acted to be standing round hearkening to him; and he will sit for all those. I heard him say he has acted in all a hundred and twenty characters and out of these the most remarkable are to be chosen.[21]

The project perhaps proved too ambitious, and nothing transpired. Aileen Ribeiro notes that Garrick's vandyke costume is trimmed with tinsel braid 'for greater dramatic impact (and to aid visibility on the stage)'. [22]

RB

30 Valentine Green (1739–1813) after Johan Zoffany (1733–1810)

***David Garrick with Mrs. Pritchard as Macbeth and Lady Macbeth**, 1776*
Mezzotint Engraving, 41.9 × 55 cm
Trustees of the British Museum
INSCRIBED *J. Zoffany Pinxit. Published March 30th, 1776, by J. Boydell. Engraver, in Cheapside, London. V. Green, Engraver to his Majesty, fecit.*
MR. GARRICK AND MRS. PRITCHARD IN THE TRAGEDY OF MACBETH, ACT II, SCENE III.

This is the moment when Macbeth, having just murdered Duncan, is confronted by his wife:

> Go get some water,
> And wash this filthy witness from your hand.
> Why did you bring these daggers from the place?

21. Shearer West, *The Image of the Actor*, London 1991, p. 42.

22. Nicholas Penny (ed.), *Reynolds* (exhibition catalogue, Royal Academy of Arts), London 1986, no. 69, p. 236.

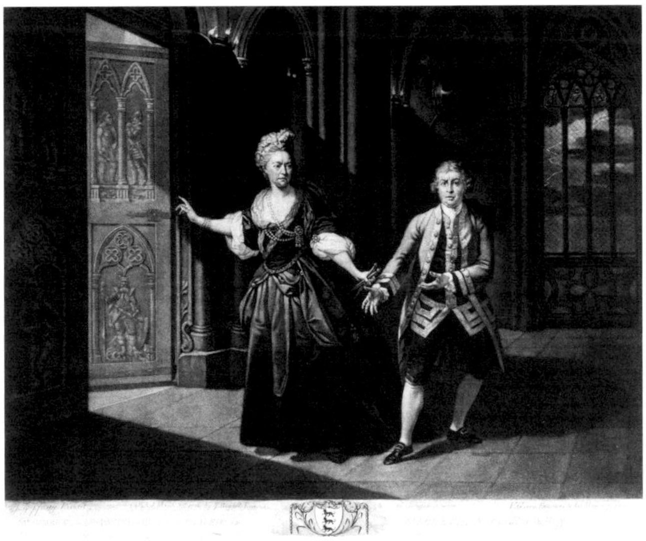

30 **Valentine Green**
after Johan Zoffany
David Garrick as Macbeth
Trustees of the British Museum.

> They must lie there: go carry them; and smear
> The sleepy grooms with blood.

Garrick appeared in contemporary costume, but after seeing Zoffany's portrait, Joseph Knight wrote that Garrick looked 'like a little man disguised as a footman'.[23] Garrick had acknowledged that he might well be considered unsuited to the role of Macbeth. He published an anonymous pamphlet before his debut in the role in 1744, lengthily entitled *An Essay on Acting: In which will be considered The Mimical behaviour of a Certain fashionable faulty Actor, and the Laudableness of such unmannerly, as well as inhumane Proceedings. To which will be added, A short Criticism on his acting Macbeth*, it anticipates any possible criticism:

> Valour and Ambition, the two Grand Characteristicks of Macbeth, form in the Mind's Eye a Person of near six Feet High, corpulently Graceful, a round Visage, a Large Hazel Eye, Acquiline Nose, prominent Chest, and a well-calv'd Leg, rather inclin'd to that which is call'd an Irish Leg; this, I say would be the Painter's Choice, was he to give us the Macbeth of his Imagination; I mention this only to prove that Mr G——k is not form'd in the least, externally, no more than internally, for that Character

Since 1664 *Macbeth* had been produced in the version revised by Sir William Davenant. The playbills for Garrick's performance emphasized that this production was 'As Written by Shakespeare'. However, Garrick could not resist creating a new dying speech for Macbeth, allowing him scope to perform his excellent 'convulsive throes and dying agonies'.[24] Mrs Pritchard was considered the greatest Lady Macbeth of her generation, and she had been Garrick's favoured stage partner for twenty-five years:

> The representation of this terrible part of the play, by Garrick and Mrs Pritchard, can no more be described than I believe it can be equalled...the merits of both were transcendent.[25]

23. Ian McIntyre, *Garrick*, London 1999, p. 84n.

24. Thomas Davies, *Dramatic Miscellanies*, 3 vols., London 1784, II, p. 118.

25. Thomas Davies, Ibid., II, p. 148.

The original painting (Baroda Museum, India), was probably painted to commemorate her final performance in 1768. She retired to Bath, but died there only a few months later, the sad news relayed to Garrick in a letter from Gainsborough. The distinctive Gothic arches and carved doorway are stylistic elements not normally found in Zoffany's work, indicating that the background reproduces the original stage set. At the time of the engraving, the painting was in the possession of the writer and artist George Keate (1729-97). RB

31 John Lodge (d. 1796)

***Mr Garrick delivering his Ode, at Drury Lane Theatre, on dedicating a Building & erecting a Statue to Shakespeare**, 1769*

Engraving, 17 × 10.7 cm

Trustees of the British Museum

INSCRIBED *J. Lodge delin et sculp. / To him the Song, the Edifice we raise, He merits all our Wonder, all our praise. / The Ode, Page* 2.

Garrick wrote and delivered this Ode as part of the Shakespeare Jubilee, a festival he organised in Stratford-upon-Avon in 1769. The Jubilee had been a disappointment to Garrick; rain had marred many of the activities he had carefully planned, including pageants, fireworks and dances. The Ode, however, was considered one of the high points of the proceedings. Garrick spoke it over accompanying music specially composed by Dr Arne:

To what blest genius of the isle,
Shall Gratitude her tribute pay,
Decree the festive day,
Erect the statue, and devote the pile?...
'Tis he! 'tis he!
The god of our idolatry!

The artist Benjamin Wilson suggested Garrick perform the Ode and adapt the pageant for Drury Lane. It was produced there for the first time on 30 September 1769, and Garrick had his statue of Shakespeare by Roubiliac brought up from his Shakespeare Temple at Hampton. This is the only known print showing Garrick with his audience at Drury Lane during his time there as manager, and before the theatre was remodelled by the Adam brothers in 1775. RB

32 Thomas Davies

***Shakespeare Casket**, 1768*

Mulberry Wood and silver, 14 cm high

The Trustees of the British Museum

The Corporation of Stratford had persuaded Garrick to present them with three works of art: a portrait of Garrick by Gainsborough, a portrait of Shakespeare by Benjamin Wilson, and a sculpture of Shakespeare by John Cheere after Scheemakers, to grace the newly built town hall in Stratford (see cat. no. 33).

After Garrick responded positively to their overtures, the Corporation commissioned the well-known Birmingham wood-carver Thomas Davies to make this casket, which contained the freedom of Stratford-upon-Avon:

> David Garrick Esqr. the greatest theatrical Genius of the Age and who has done the highest Honors to the Memory of the immortal Shakespeare (a Native of this place) was unanimously elected an honorary Burgess of this Corporation, and his freedom was directed to be presented to him in a Box to be made of the Mulberry Tree planted by Shakespeare's own hand.

The casket apparently took Davies four months of 'constant application'. Garrick was honoured:

> The Freedom of your Town given to me unanimously, sent to me in such an elegant and estimable Box, and deliver'd to me in so flattering a Manner merit my warmest gratitude.

The front of the casket shows Fame presenting a bust of Shakespeare to the three Graces. The reverse shows Garrick as Lear, on the storm-blasted heath, after Wilson's portrait of the same scene; Davies probably used McArdell's print (cat. no. 13) as reference for this carving. The short sides are carved with putti representing tragedy and comedy. The feet of the casket represent silver dragons, with garnet eyes and enamelled barbed tongues. RB

33 After Thomas Gainsborough (1727–1788)

***David Garrick with a bust of Shakespeare**, early 19th century*

Oil on canvas, 113.5 × 75.5 cm

Charlecote Park, The Fairfax Lucy Collection (The National Trust)

The original, life-size, version of this portrait was destroyed in a fire at Stratford Town Hall in 1946. Garrick is probably shown in the garden of Prior Park, the estate at Bath belonging to Gainsborough's patron Ralph Allen, where he and Garrick had both spent time as guests. The portrait was exhibited at the Society of Artists, and was entitled *A Gentleman Whole Length*.

In December 1768 the Corporation of Stratford invited Garrick to furnish their new town hall with 'some statue Bust or Picture' of Shakespeare, and also 'some Picture of yourself that the Memory of both may be perpetuated together'. Gainsborough's portrait, which shows Garrick embracing the bust of his hero like an old friend, had been completed in 1766 and must have struck Garrick as being particularly suited to the wording of this commission, which closely associates Garrick and Shakespeare.

Garrick's cross-legged pose derives from the famous full-length statue of Shakespeare by Scheemakers in Westminster Abbey. Garrick had subscribed to the fund to erect this memorial in 1740, the year before he made his debut in *Richard III*.[26] The pose was also used by Roubiliac when sculpting Shakespeare for Garrick's Temple at Hampton in 1758, for which Garrick modelled. This portrait is a more developed and dynamic representation of the concept of Shakespeare's inspiration than Gainborough had previously employed. When painting another actor, James Quin, in 1763, Gainsborough included a bust of Shakespeare in the background as an allusion to the profession from which Quin had retired (National Gallery

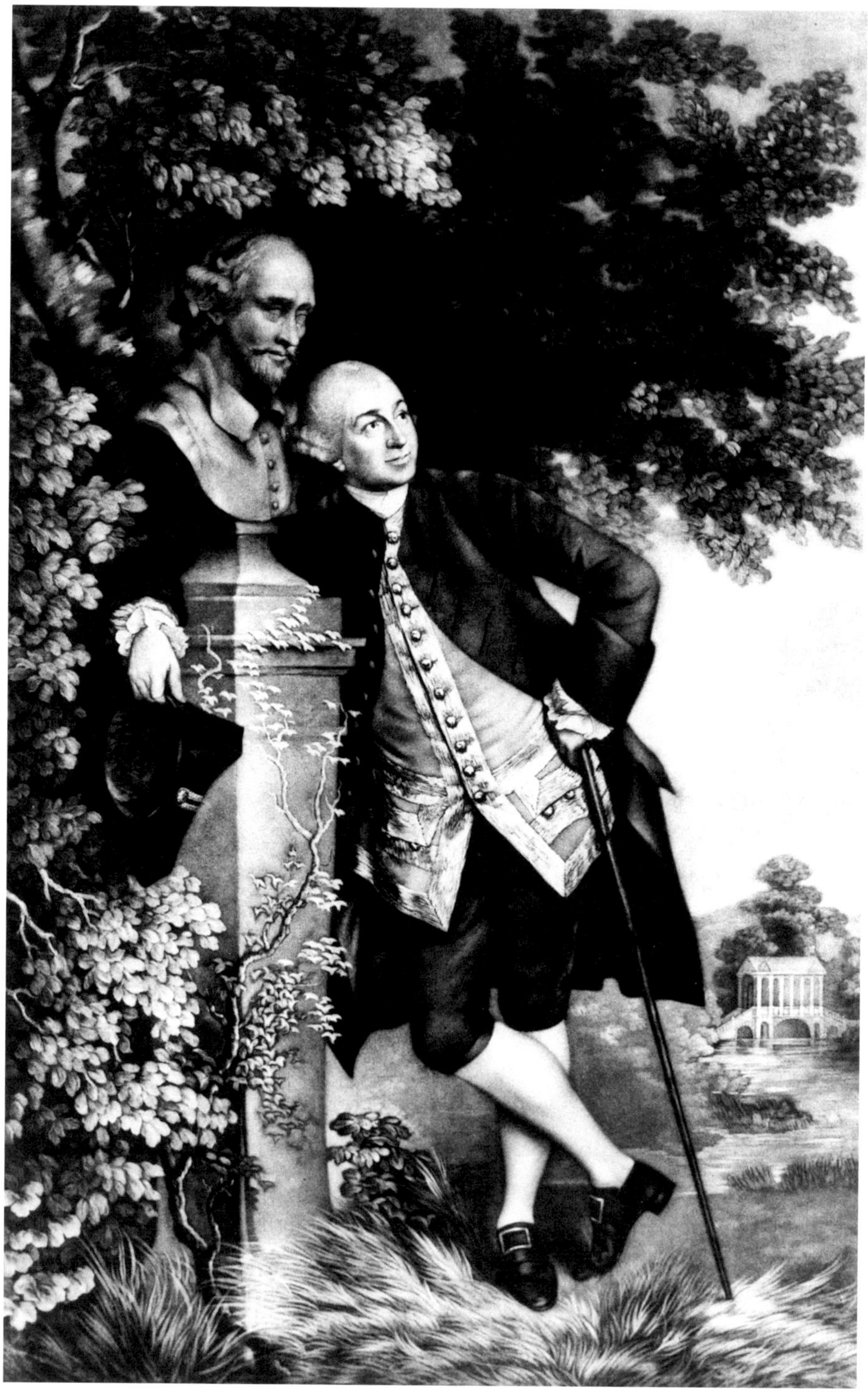

34 Valentine Green
after Thomas Gainsborough
David Garrick Esq.
David Alexander.

of Ireland). By painting Garrick in a pose traditional to representations of Shakespeare, Gainsborough further compounds the association between poet and actor. Garrick never owned Gainsborough's portrait himself, but seems to have acted as an agent for Gainsborough, asking him to re-work the picture for the Corporation, who paid the artist 60 guineas.

This copy now hangs in the library at Charlecote, the Lucy family estate on the river Avon, not very far from Stratford Town Hall, where the original portrait hung. According to legend,

26. Alan Kendall, *David Garrick, A Biography*, London 1985, pp.19–20.

the young Shakesepeare was caught poaching deer on the Charlecote estate, and had been severely reprimanded by Sir Thomas Lucy, who was later to be Shakespeare's model for Justice Shallow in *The Merry Wives of Windsor*. The legend was well established by the eighteenth century, and Shakespeare and the Lucy family were reconciled at the Shakespeare Festival of 1769. George Lucy (1714-1788) acted as a kind of Master of Ceremonies for the festivities, in his capacity as Lord High Sheriff of Warwickshire. He encouraged visitors to take excursions to Charlecote, in order to examine the site of the poaching incident.[27] This painting is an early nineteenth-century copy, which may have been commissioned by George's descendant George Hammond Lucy (1789–1845); the frame is of the type he used for paintings in his new library. Another possibility is that it was commissioned by George Hammond's widow Mary Elizabeth (1803–1890), the chatelaine of Charlecote when the centenary of Garrick's first Shakespeare Jubilee was celebrated. RB

34 Valentine Green (1739–1813) after Thomas Gainsborough (1727–1788)

David Garrick Esq., *1769*
Mezzotint Engraving, 60 × 37.5 cm
David Alexander
Finished proof before all letters, the inscription space grounded

This print was published by John Boydell on 2nd April 1769. Thomas Becket, the established bookseller on the Strand in London, advertised in *The London Chronicle* in 1769 that he would be selling:

> A fine Metzotinto Print (done from a Capital painting of Mr Gainsborough) now in the Great Hall at Stratford, of Mrs [sic] Garrick, with a bust of Shakespeare[...][28]

In addition to this portrait of Garrick with a bust of Shakespeare, Martin Postle has shown that Garrick also commissioned Gainsborough to paint a portrait of *Shakespeare between Tragedy and Comedy*, probably to fulfil the first part of the commission from the Corporation, for a 'statue bust or picture' of Shakespeare.[29] Garrick was proactive as usual, involving himself with the conception of the painting, suggesting Gainsborough use the engraved portrait of Shakespeare from the first Folio, or a bust in Stratford, as the basis for the portrait. However, Gainsborough responded that the bust was a 'silly smiling thing', and that he had never beheld a 'stupider face' than the engraving. Gainsborough wanted to show something of Shakespeare's genius and inspiration 'by an immediate Ray darting down upon his Eye turn'd up for the purpose'.[30]

However, by late August, Gainsborough had abandoned the project, telling Garrick that he could not see the picture. Instead, Garrick provided the Corporation with a portrait of Shakespeare (also destroyed by fire), which he commissioned from Benjamin Wilson (who was acting as a general artistic advisor for the Jubilee), and a copy of Scheemaker's statue of Shakespeare by the sculptor John Cheere (1709–1787). Gainsborough's attempted portrait of Shakespeare has been discovered by x-ray beneath his portrait of Johan Christian Fischer (1780, The Royal Collection). RB

27. Clive Wainwright, *The Romantic Interior*, London 1989, pp. 209–211.

28. Christopher Lennox-Boyd, G. Shaw, S. Halliwell, *Theatre: in the Age of Garrick. English mezzotints from the collection of the Hon. Christopher Lennox-Boyd* (exhibition catalogue, Courtauld Institute Galleries), London 1994, p. 110.

29. Martin Postle, 'Gainsborough's 'lost' picture of Shakespeare', *Apollo*, December 1991, pp.374–79.

30. See Desmond Shawe-Taylor, *Genial Company: The Theme of genius in Eighteenth-Century British Portraiture*, (exhibition catalogue, Nottingham University Art Gallery and Scottish National Portrait Gallery), Nottingham 1987, pp. 50–52.

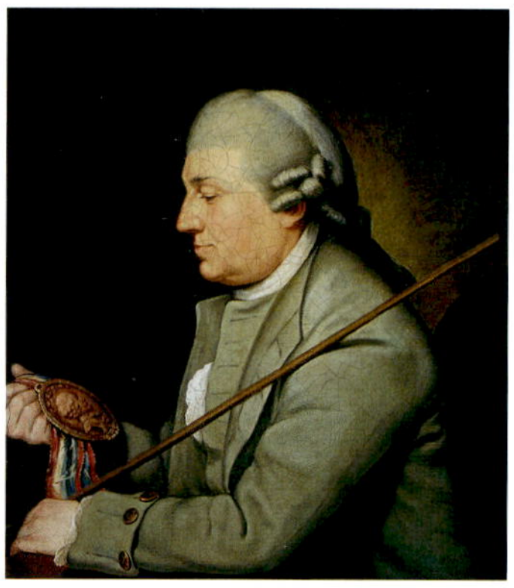

35 **After Benjamin Van der Gucht**
David Garrick with the Shakespeare Jubliee Medal.
By Courtesy of the Trustees of the Samuel Johnson Birthplace Museum.

35 After Benjamin Van der Gucht (1753–1794)

David Garrick with the Shakespeare Jubilee Medal, 1772
Oil on canvas, 73.8 × 64.2 cm
By Courtesy of the Trustees of the Samuel Johnson Birthplace Museum

Garrick is shown holding his Jubilee Medal (Shakespeare Birthplace Museum), made, like Thomas Davies' casket (cat. no. 32) from the wood of Shakespeare's famous mulberry tree. Garrick wore it to conduct his duties as Steward of the Shakespeare Jubilee of 1769.

In July 1777 Van der Gucht was travelling on the continent and corresponding with Garrick, who requested from him various books, including accounts of the Parisian theatre, works of Classical authors and any theatrical pamphlets 'wch make a Noise'. Garrick admired Van der Gucht's descriptive powers: 'you draw & colour, as well with y^r pen as with y^r brush'. Garrick proposed that Van der Gucht paint the country parson he had described in a previous letter; 'you must put him on canvas – I see him running up & down, with a face of fear, rage and despair', another example of Garrick's delight in suggesting ideas to painters.

The original version of this portrait now hangs at Althorp. It was exhibited at the Royal Academy and was one of a number of theatrical portraits painted by Van der Gucht, who also painted theatrical conversation pieces, influenced by Zoffany. He gave up painting in 1787 to become a picture cleaner and dealer, and died in 1796 in a boating accident on the Thames. RB

36 Johan Zoffany (1733-1810)

Two sketches for ***David Garrick as Abel Drugger in Jonson's 'The Alchymist'****, 1769–70*
Oil on canvas, 33 × 38 cm
Ashmolean Museum, Oxford, Chambers Hall Gift, 1855

These studies were made in preparation for Zoffany's famous painting of Garrick with Mr Burton and Mr Palmer in *The Alchymist* (Private collection, see fig. 9). Abel Drugger, a tobacconist, is one of the many characters who are duped by the man-servant Face and his partner, the bogus alchemist Subtle. Garrick transformed the way in which Drugger had previously been portrayed, particularly by the actor Theophilus Cibber, who relied upon 'absurd grimaces'. Garrick was far more understated:

> The moment he came upon the stage, he discovered such awkward simplicity, and his looks so happily bespoke the ignorant, selfish, and absurd tobacco-merchant ... Through the whole part he strictly preserved the modesty of nature.

What is evident in these sketches is the physical approach Garrick took to the role, seeming to 'become' this lowly tobacconist. That a grocer from Garrick's home town of Lichfield believed that Garrick really was Drugger, is testament to his success. The grocer was visiting London armed with a letter of introduction from Garrick's brother Peter, arriving at the theatre during a performance of *The Alchymist*. When he returned to Lichfield he told Peter Garrick why he had decided not to approach the actor:

> I saw enough of him on the stage to make that unnecessary. He may be rich, as I dare say any man who lives like him must be; but by G-d, though he is your brother, Mr. Garrick, he is one of the shabbiest, meanest, most pitiful hounds I ever saw in the whole course of my life.[31]

31. Thomas Davies, *Memoirs of a Life of David Garrick*, 2 vols., London 1808, I, p. 61.

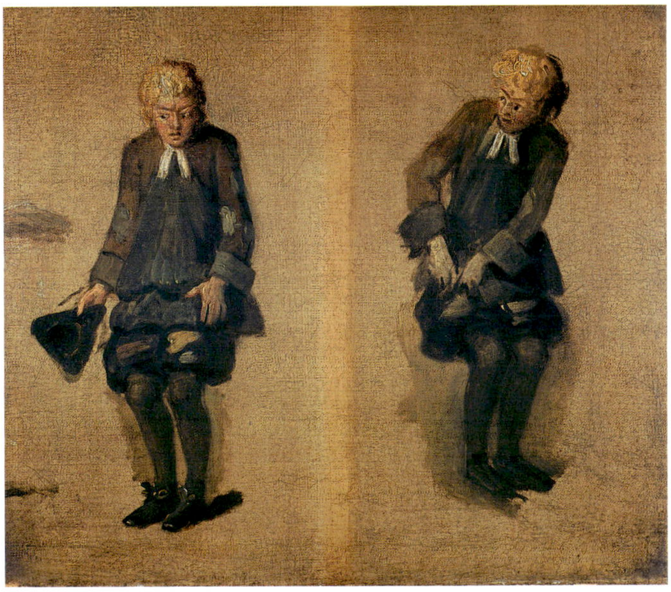

36 Johan Zoffany
Two sketches for David Garrick in 'The Alchymist'
The Ashmolean Museum, Oxford.

Zoffany's apparent alacrity in executing these sketches indicates that they may have been made during a rehearsal. If this was the case, then speed was certainly necessary, because Garrick only occupied the stage briefly in this role, despite the enormous impact he made. A year after Garrick first appeared as Abel Drugger he published, anonymously, a short essay on acting. He described his approach to this role:

> His toes must be *inverted* from the Heel, and by *holding* his *Breath*, he will unavoidably give himself a *Tremor* in the *Knees*, and if his *Fingers*, at the same Time, seem *Convuls'd*, it finishes the compleatest low Picture of *Grotesque Terror* that can be imagin'd by a *Dutch* painter.

Zoffany did not use either of these poses directly in his completed picture, but the comical air and sideways glance, the slouching pose and ill-fitting suit, were all translated to the final work. RB

37 Chitqua (also known as Shykingqua) (d. 1796)

called David Garrick, 1769–1771
Painted clay
Private Collection

It is not certain that Garrick ever sat to the Cantonese sculptor Chitqua, but the pose of this figure of the actor perhaps derives from Zoffany's portrait of Mr and Mrs Garrick at the Shakespeare Temple (cat. no. 16). Chitqua came to England in August 1769, where he achieved considerable fame for his realistic miniature figure sculptures. This sculpture was perhaps speculative, made soon after Chitqua's arrival England, in the knowledge that depicting such a well-known figure would draw attention to his work.

Very soon, distinguished patrons were eager to sit to him, including the King and Queen. In these sculptures, every detail of the sitters' clothes and hair was exquisitely rendered. When William Hickey sat to Chitqua, he was careful to wear his most decorative suit of clothes,

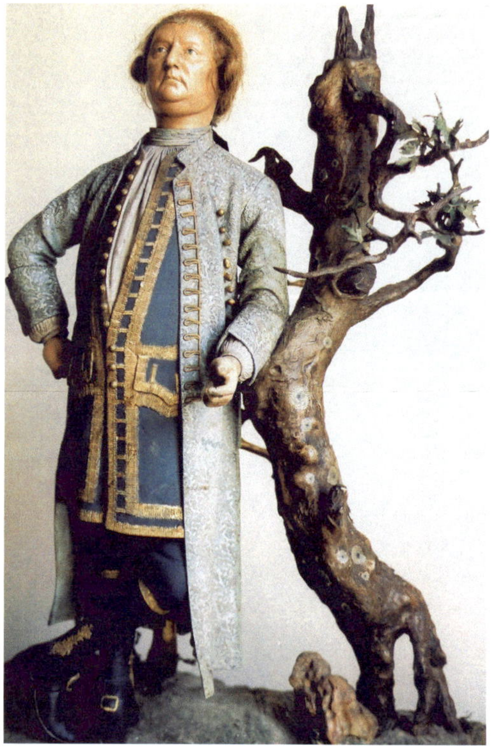

37 **Chitqua**
David Garrick
Private Collection.

knowing that his outfit would be carefully reproduced.[33] Chitqua may have been made aware of Garrick through Zoffany, who chose to include the foreign visitor in his portrait of the distinguished members of the Royal Academy (Royal Collection), shortly before his return to China in 1771.

RB

38 Thomas Gainsborough (1727–1788)

David Garrick, 1770–71
Oil on canvas 81.5 × 76 cm
Private Collection

Gainsborough painted three 'head' sized (30 × 25 inch) portraits of Garrick between 1770 and 1772. The first, exhibited at the Royal Academy in 1770 (n.86) is believed to be the version now in the National Portrait Gallery. The portrait exhibited here, completed by May 1771, is the version painted for Garrick's financial adviser and friend James Clutterbuck; the third (presumably the canvas to which Gainsborough refers in a letter of 22 June 1772) was sold at Sotheby's, London, on 18 November 1981 (lot 184). In a letter to Garrick, the artist writes:

> I never will consent that any body makes a present of your face to Clutterbuck but myself, because I always intended a Copy (by my own hand) for Him, that he may one day tell me what to do with my Money, the only thing he understands except jeering at folks.[34]

The portrait does appear to be by Gainsborough's 'own hand' and, like the first version, beautifully expresses Garrick's personality through his twinkling eyes and half smile. The actor

33. Carl C. Crossman, *The China Trade*, Suffolk 1991, p. 314.

34. John Hayes (ed.), *The Letters of Thomas Gainsborough*, London 2001, no. 62, p. 105.

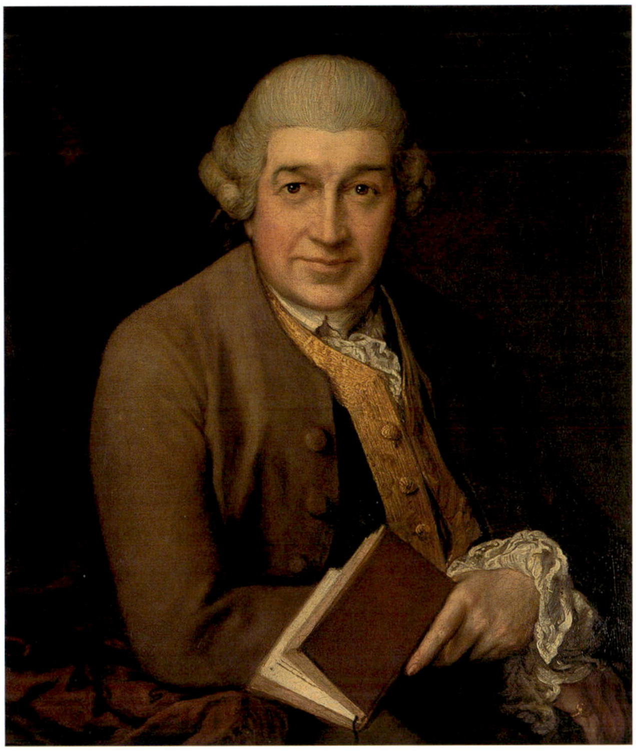

38 Thomas Gainsborough
David Garrick
Private Collection.

seems to be leaning forward out of the picture space and looks directly at the viewer; hence the artist's advice to hang the original version 'breast high' (see p. 28). Only the white shirt and lace cuff of the Clutterbuck *Garrick* seem to be finished or overpainted by a different hand. Clutterbuck's gratitude to Gainsborough, and his admiration for the portrait are spelled out in a letter to Garrick dated 4 May 1771.[35] Despite Gainsborough's comment about Clutterbuck's 'jeering', the two men were probably friends, and Clutterbuck was the brother-in-law of John Jacob, one of the artist's early Bath patrons.[36]

James Clutterbuck (1704?–1776) began trading as a 'man's mercer' at 157 Strand, London in 1735. Around 1745 he expanded into the shop next door and by 1759 the business, known as Clutterbuck and Gastrell, was one of the largest on the Strand. The firm was a supplier to the Drury Lane Theatre. In common with many other mercers and drapers, Clutterbuck provided banking and financial management services. The original shop sign of the Three Angels may have been a tribute to the three sisters of John Jacob who are referred to as 'the Three Angells' in a letter written by Clutterbuck to their uncle in 1739 (Private Collection). James Clutterbuck and Mary Jacob (1713–1790) enjoyed a long and happy marriage and Mary was an affectionate friend of Garrick's wife. Latterly they rented Lucknam Park near Bath from Paul Methuen of Corsham and then Claverton Manor, Bath, from the heirs of Ralph Allen of Prior Park. (Both Methuen and Allen were also patrons of Gainsborough). James Clutterbuck was evidently closely related to Bath's long-serving Town Clerk Lewis Clutterbuck (d. 1776), since both families were buried in the small churchyard at Claverton, although Lewis lived outside that parish, at Widcombe. James and Mary Clutterbuck had no children and their pictures passed to Mary's sister Elizabeth Buxton and, happily, have remained together in the same family collection to the present day.

SS

35. partly published by William T. Whitley, *Thomas Gainsborough*, 1915, p. 82.

36 see Susan Sloman, *Gainsborough in Bath*, London 2002, pp. 177–79.

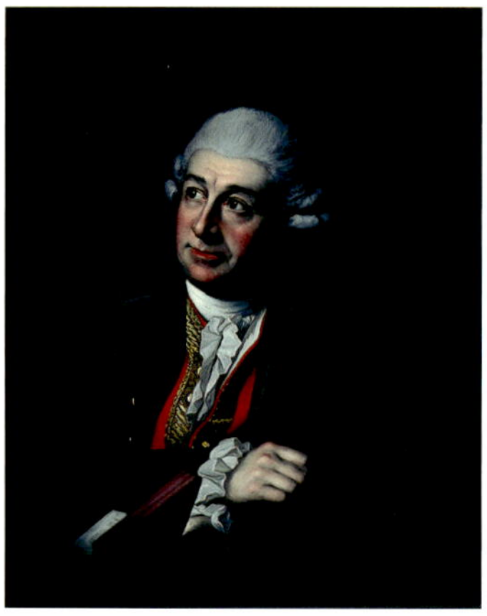

Fig.12 Nathaniel Dance (1735–1811)
***David Garrick**, 1774*, **oil on canvas**
76.2 × 63.8 cm
The Folger Shakespeare Library, Washington D.C.

39 Nathaniel Dance (1735–1811)

***David Garrick**, 1771*
Pencil, 13.6 × 11.4 cm
National Portrait Gallery, London
INSCRIBED verso: *drawn by Dance of* [sic] *the breakfast Table//These two pencil drawings by Dance – hung up in Garrick's study – and at Mrs Garrick's death passed to Mrs J. G. Payne – née Garrick his niece – and at Mrs Paynes death came into the possession of her Godchild Miss Desirée D'Enville – my first wife – Mr Garrick always considered it the best likeness ever made of him. Mrs Garrick, née Violette is in her night cap./ W.E. Image/ Herringswell/ House* [Mildenhall, Suffolk].
(Illustrated on p.6)

This drawing has a pendant, a portrait of Mrs Garrick, formerly at the National Portrait Gallery (stolen 1968). According to tradition, Dance executed these drawings while at the Garricks' breakfast table. The drawing of Mrs Garrick is dated 16th March 1771, made at the time Dance was finishing his full-length portrait of Garrick as Richard III (see cat. no. 41). When Garrick moved to the Adelphi Terrace in 1772, he hung Dance's drawing in the library. The inscription notes that Mrs Garrick thought this to be the 'best likeness' ever made of her husband. Several portraits share this distinction, including Gainsborough's portrait of Garrick with the bust of Shakespeare (see cat. no.s 33 and 34), which she also considered the 'best likeness of my Davy'.

Dance and Garrick met in Rome in 1764, when Garrick was sitting to Pompeo Batoni (cat. no. 25). By 1762, Dance had become a partner in Batoni's extremely successful portraiture business. He told his father, 'I am now in such a situation in Rome that I cannot fail of making acquaintance with some of the greatest people in England'.[37] Garrick sat for both artists, as noted by Walpole in April 1764, but a portrait by Dance from this time has not been identified with certainty. Garrick wrote of Dance, 'the painter is a great Genius, and will do w^{t} he pleases when he goes to London'.

This drawing was the basis of an untraced portrait in oil, which was in the collection of William Murray, 1st Earl of Mansfield. An engraving of the oil portrait, by John Hall, was published on 1st December 1773. Dance painted another version of this portrait for Garrick, which Garrick gave to his friend the landscape artist John Taylor of Bath in 1774 (Folger Shakespeare Library, Washington DC, fig. 11). Taylor's opinion on Dance's ability to capture Garrick's likeness concurs with that of Mrs Garrick. The painting is inscribed on the front:

> Anno 1774. This Portrait of my dear & worthy friend DAVID GARRICK Esqr. (Painted by Mr. N. Dance of London) was presented to me by Himself, & is in my own opinion, as well as every other person's, allow'd to be the most true & striking likeness of that great Man, that ever was painted. John Taylor.

Taylor and Garrick had become friends in Bath, through Thomas Gainsborough, Taylor's neighbour in the Circus. In Bath, Garrick viewed a public display of Taylor's landscapes, and wrote a verse comparing Taylor to Claude Lorrain, which received wide circulation.

Taylor presented Garrick with one of his own paintings, described in Garrick's inventory

37. *Nathaniel Dance* 1735 – 1811 (exhibition catalogue, The Iveagh Bequest, Kenwood), London 1977, p. 4.

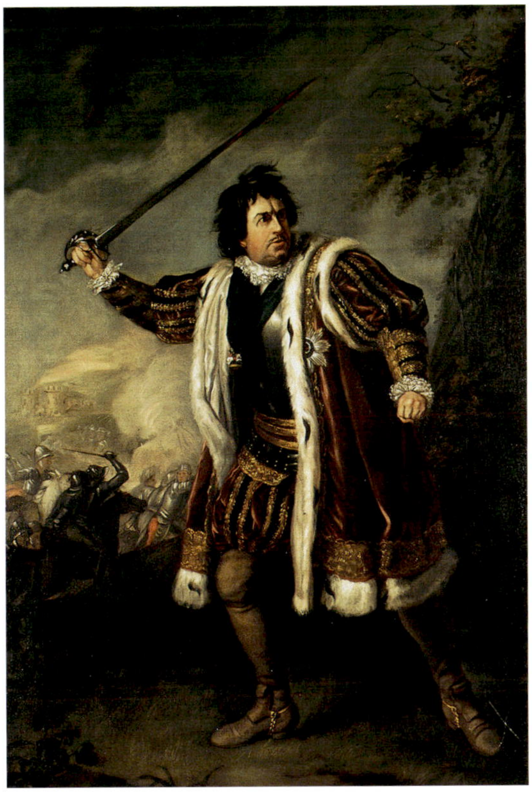

40 Henry Robert Morland
after Nathaniel Dance
David Garrick as Richard III
The Art Archive/Garrick Club.

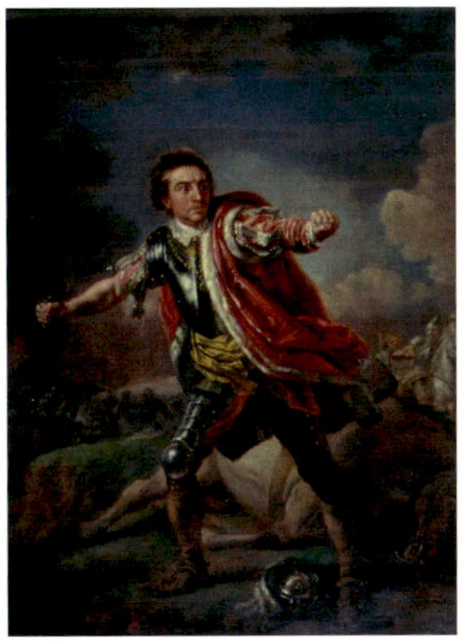

FIG. 13 Francis Hayman (1708–1776)
David Garrick as Richard III, 1760,
oil on canvas, 89.5 × 64.1 cm
Somerset Maugham Collection of Theatrical Paintings, Royal National Theatre.

as 'An oval landscape, with Buildings, Water , and figures'. This exchange is another example of Garrick's practice of giving portraits of himself as tokens of friendship, similar to the exchange of portraits arranged between Garrick and Quin (see cat. no. 5), and the exchange of works of art between Garrick and the Rev. Richard Kaye in Rome (see cat. no. 25). Garrick hung Taylor's landscape in his dining room at Hampton, he thought it a 'most exquisite piece of painting' and enthused, 'We have scarcely look'd at anything Else till this moment, ... our wishes are fullfill'd by it, and our Expectations Exceeded – It makes a most Noble figure.'[38] RB

40 Henry Robert Morland (1719?–1797) after Nathaniel Dance (1735–1811)

David Garrick as Richard III

Oil on canvas, 87 × 58.4 cm

The Garrick Club

This is one of the many copies of the popular portrait by Nathaniel Dance (whom Garrick had met in Rome in 1764; see cat. no. 39), exhibited at the Royal Academy in 1771, and which now hangs in the Town Hall in Stratford-upon-Avon. Dance had been a pupil of Hayman (cat. no. 7), and this picture is a response to Hayman's portrait of Garrick in the same role a decade earlier (Maugham Collection, National Theatre). Dance has chosen the same scene as Hayman (Fig. 13) and has also placed Garrick in a real setting, as if actually at Bosworth, and as though this were a history painting rather than a theatrical scene.

Garrick played the part of Richard throughout his career, but as he matured he found the role an increasing physical challenge. Garrick told his friend Cradock, 'I can play Richard, but I dread the fight and the fall. I am afterwards in agonies', and before his final performance, he

38. Arthur S. Marks, 'An Eighteenth-century American landscape painter rediscovered: John Taylor of Bath', *The American Art Journal*, November 1978, pp. 81–96.

confided to Hannah More: 'it will absolutely kill me – what a trial of breast, lungs, ribs and what not.' This feeling seems to be reflected in Dance's portrait, where Garrick is less dynamic than Hayman's earlier depiction, which uses a pose based on a classical statue, the Borghese Gladiator. Dance places the emphasis on Garrick's stature rather than his agility.

The pose Dance employs is based on a later source: an engraving after a Poussin drawing of a man throwing a spear, published in a French edition of Leonardo da Vinci's *Trattato della Pittura*, in the mid-seventeenth century (fig. 5). In fact, Garrick may well have been inspired by such Classical and Renaissance sources when devising his own performance. The actor and manager Thomas Betterton, whom Garrick admired, had himself advised actors to model their poses and attitudes on statues and paintings:

> The studying History-Painting would be very useful because the knowledge of the Figure and Lineaments of the persons represented will teach the Actor to vary and change his Figure.[39]

The original painting hung in the drawing room of 20 St. James's Square, London, home of Sir Watkin Williams Wynne, who paid one hundred and fifty guineas for it (see also cat. no. 70). The portrait received a large audience. Eileen Harris states that 'entertainment was what the house was for' and the drawing room was part of a very public suite of rooms known as an *appartement de parade.*[40] It was engraved as a mezzotint by John Dixon in 1772, and Morland may have based his copy on this print. The figure was also produced by the Derby and Staffordshire potteries.

RB

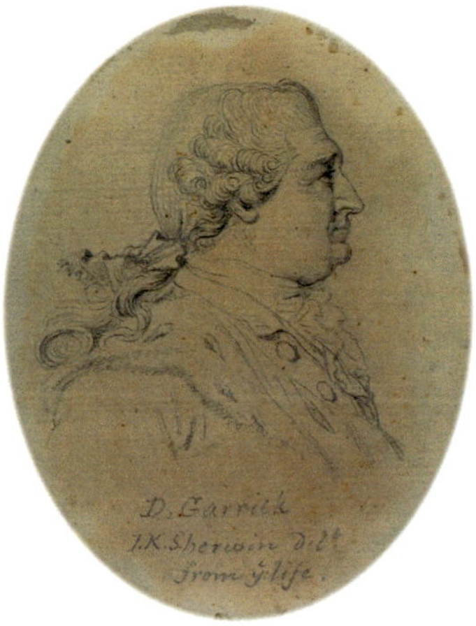

41 John Keyse Sherwin
David Garrick
By courtesy of the National Portrait Gallery, London.

41 John Keyse Sherwin (1751–1790)

David Garrick, c. 1774
Pencil, 8.9 × 7 cm
National Portrait Gallery, London.
INSCRIPTION *D. Garrick/I.K Sherwin Del^t./from ye life.*

A label on the frame verso: *This is Sherwin's original drawing from/ which he engraved* [a] *print.* The extent of Garrick's fame and popularity undoubtedly created a demand for small-scale portraits of Garrick, which were cheaper and easier to accommodate than a large picture or bust, but were suitably heroic. This sort of profile portrait is associated with the concept of 'eternal fame', derived as it is from Antique coins and medals, and is usually reserved for portraits of kings or poets. In the later part of his life several profile portraits of Garrick were produced (cat. no.s 35, 60 and 61). It was acknowledged that many of Garrick's performances could never be recorded for posterity, but Garrick was being accorded the same honour as a poet whose works would be read by future generations. Garrick wrote plays, prologues and verse, and this type of portrait may be a tribute to this work, but it is also an acknowledgement that he had raised acting to a liberal art in the eyes of his contemporaries.

Sherwin, a draughtsman and engraver, copied this drawing of Garrick as an engraving. This profile compares with the wax medallion carved by Lewis Pingo in 1772, used as a pattern for a Wedgwood medallion in 1773 (cat. no. 60). Sherwin had studied under Francesco Bartolozzi (1727–1815) at the Royal Academy Schools and was appointed historical engraver to the King in 1785.

RB

39. Ronald Paulson, *Hogarth: His Life, Art, and Times*, 2 Vols., London 1971, II, p .26.

40. Eileen Harris, *The Genius of Robert Adam: His Interiors*, London 2001, p. 259.

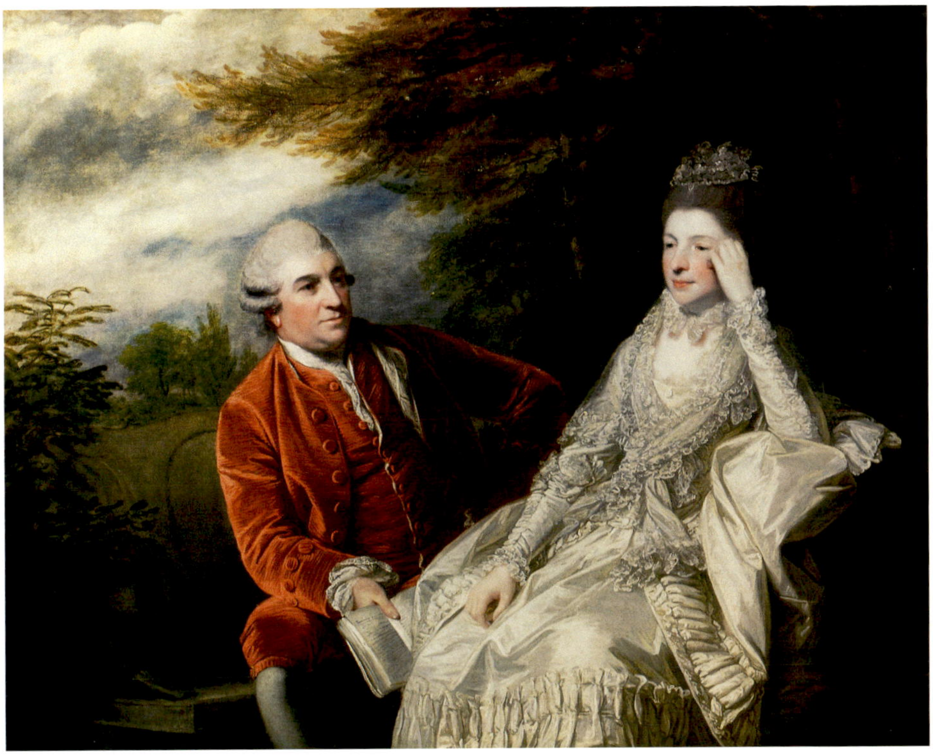

42 Sir Joshua Reynolds
David Garrick reading to his wife Eva Maria
By courtesy of the National Portrait Gallery, London.

42 Sir Joshua Reynolds (1723–1792)
David Garrick reading to his wife Eva Maria, 1773
Oil on canvas, 139.5 × 169 cm
National Portrait Gallery, London.

Garrick and Eva Maria had been married for twenty-four years when they sat for this portrait. By all accounts, the Garricks enjoyed a very happy marriage, although their childlessness had caused them some sorrow. Mrs Garrick devoted herself to being a hostess and created beautiful decorative schemes at their house, particularly the villa at Hampton (see cat. no.s 54–57). Garrick is said to have relied on his wife's opinion and advice in many areas of his work. When Garrick died, Mrs Garrick took the news very calmly: 'Groans and complaints are very well for those who are to mourn but a little while' she remarked, 'but a sorrow which is to last for life will not be violent and romantic'. She lived as a widow at Hampton, for a further forty-three years.

This portrait was commissioned by Garrick's friend The Hon. Thomas FitzMaurice (1742-1793), brother of the Earl of Sherbourne. Garrick and his wife stayed with him at Knighton (his estate on the Isle of Wight) in July 1772, and this portrait was begun in October of the same year. FitzMaurice was himself sitting to Reynolds for a portrait that autumn (Bowood House, Wiltshire).

Both Garrick and FitzMaurice seemed to have found sitting to Reynolds rather tiresome: FitzMaurice complained that lack of company during sittings left his portrait lacking animation, and in turn Garrick, in a letter to FitzMaurice dated 19th January 1773, writes; 'I am going in a q^{r} of an hour *to Sr Josa* for the last time, I hope'. Fitzmaurice paid 150 guineas for this portrait, as recorded in Reynolds's ledger for 1775. RB

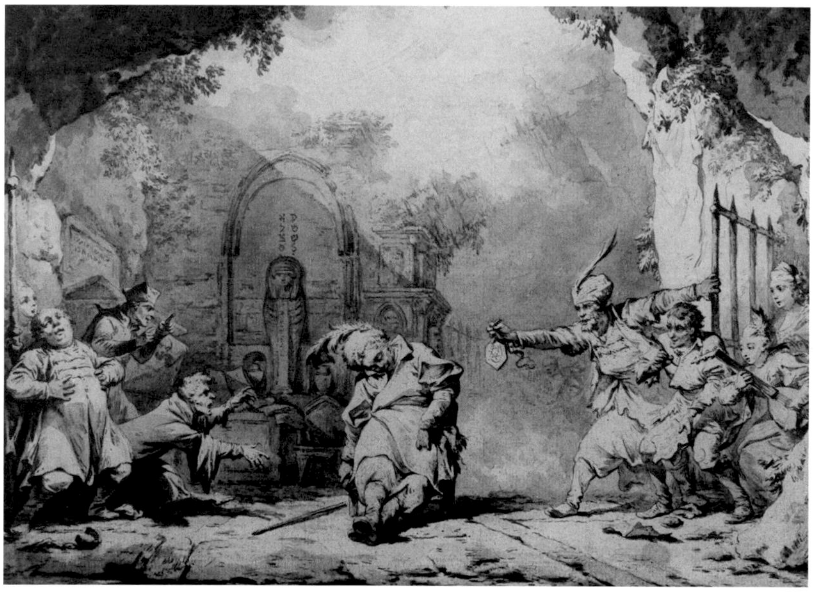

43 Philippe Jacques de Loutherbourg
Bonoro's Cell, a scene from 'A Christmas Tale'
Trustees of the late Sir Brinsley Ford.

43 Philippe Jacques de Loutherbourg (1740–1812)

Bonoro's Cell, a scene from Garrick's 'A Christmas Tale', 1773
Pencil, pen and sepia, 23 × 31 cm
Trustees of the late Sir Brinsley Ford

A Christmas Tale was produced on 27 December 1773. Garrick adapted the plot from a French comedy, chosen specifically to make use of De Loutherbourg's talents as a scene designer. The two worked together closely to devise spectacular scenes, including a burning castle and a forest where the foliage turned from green to blood red. It was the most revolutionary production of the century, employing a range of innovative technical and mechanical devices.

De Loutherbourg had obtained an introduction to Garrick in 1771, through Jean Monnet, the director of the Opera-Comique in Paris. He wrote:

> Mr. De Loutherbourg, one of our greatest painters and a very agreeable man, intends for his pleasure to make an excursion to London in the near future. He has asked me for a letter of introduction to you, and as you love all arts and artists, I have given it to him … He is not expensive and I advise you strongly to let him paint three small pictures for you, one a sea piece, another a landscape in the manner of Berghem, and thirdly a battle scene. He is delightful in all three genres.[41]

Garrick initially employed De Loutherbourg at Drury Lane in 1772 to design a pantomime called *The Pigmy Revels*. He had long been concerned with the scenic improvement of the stage and found De Loutherbourg's conception of 'harmony between the scene decoration, the costumes and the subject of the play' appealing. The collaboration between writer and designer on *A Christmas Tale* meant that this sense of harmony was achieved.

When working at Drury Lane in the 1730s and 40s (cat. no. 7), Francis Hayman established the concept of naturalistic scenery, later developed by De Loutherbourg so as to transform the stage into a picture. This drawing records the scene when Tycho, guarding a group of evil

41. Rudiger Joppien, *Philippe Jacques de Loutherbourg, RA 1740–1812* (exhibition catalogue, The Iveagh Bequest, Kenwood), London 1973, p. 2.

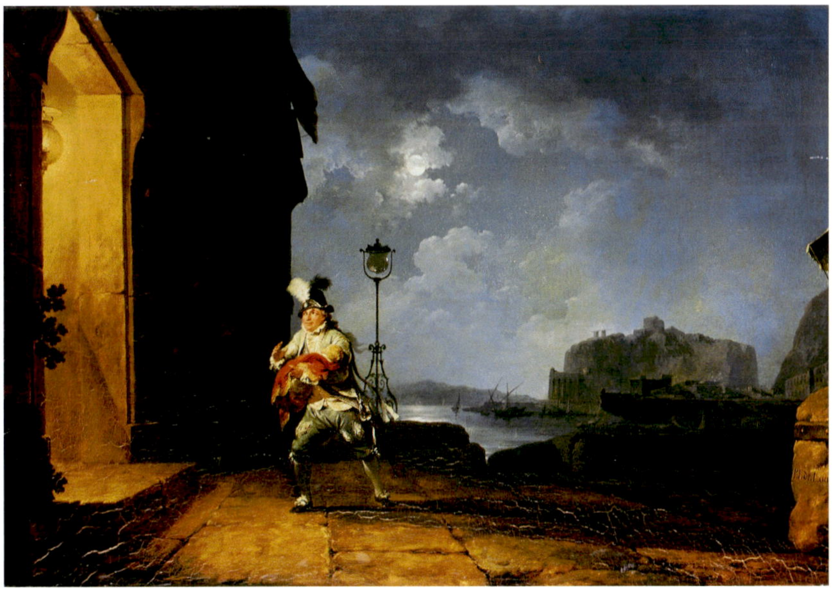

44 Philippe Jacques De Loutherbourg
David Garrick in 'The Chances'
Theatre Museum.

spirits, captured and placed in cells by his father, Bonoro, falls asleep allowing the spirits to escape. The next moment the stage is plunged into darkness, echoing with their yells and howls. This drawing shows the rock-like wings that enclose Bonoro's cell, their irregularity merging into the acting space. A dramatic shaft of light creates a suitably magical atmosphere.

Despite Horace Walpole's description of the story as 'dire', the play was published with an etching of this scene as the frontispiece. De Loutherbourg had a keen interest in publicising his achievement, and made four engravings of scenes from *A Christmas Tale,* which had established his reputation in Britain. This type of spectacle was not, however, universally admired. Gainsborough disapproved of the use of garish colours in scenery. When Garrick began to work with De Loutherbourg, Gainsborough warned him: 'when Eyes and ears are thoroughly debauch'd by Glare and noise, the returning to modest truth will seem very gloomy for a time'. RB

44 Philippe Jacques De Loutherbourg (1740–1812)

***Garrick as Don John in 'The Chances'**, 1774*

Oil on canvas, 56 × 78.6 cm

Dyce 70 Theatre Museum, Victoria and Albert Museum

INSCRIBED *P.I. de Loutherbourg* in black oil paint

The Chances, a comedy by Beaumont and Fletcher, was taken from a short story by Cervantes. This painting commemorates a new production, which opened in April 1773, 'with great Alterations by Mr. Garrick'. Don John was one of Garrick's favourite roles, and one he had played often in the 1750s. De Loutherbourg has depicted the opening scene when Don John, taking an evening stroll, is hailed by a woman from an open doorway. She thrusts a bundle into his arms, which Don John hopes contains money or jewels but is, instead, a baby:

> What Have I got by this now? – a Child!

It is not certain whether Garrick actually commissioned this work from De Loutherbourg.

He owned several De Loutherbourg landscapes, but this painting does not appear in Garrick's inventories.

Contractual negotiations meant that De Loutherbourg was not officially an employee of the theatre during the production of *The Chances*, but he was in regular contact with Garrick. It is likely that he contributed to the design of this production, and that this painting, and the atmospheric view of Naples, is a record of this project. When the painting was exhibited at the Royal Academy in 1774, the emphasis of the catalogue entry was as much on the view of Naples as the portrait of Garrick as Don John, which seems to indicate that the scenery in the production was noteworthy and, by implication, that De Loutherbourg was in some way responsible for it. De Loutherbourg also painted a watercolour of the scene (Victoria and Albert Museum). He continued to work at Drury Lane after Garrick's retirement, until his election to the Royal Academy in 1781. RB

45 Jug showing Garrick as Don John in *The Chances*, *c.* 1779

Creamware, 25.5 cm high

S1090-1996 Theatre Museum, Victoria and Albert Museum

Edward Edwards made a figure study from De Loutherbourg's painting of Garrick as Don John, which was engraved by Hall for the *New English Theatre*, published by T. Lowndes & Partners 16 September 1777. It is likely that the manufacturers used this print as the basis for the decoration of this jug, an example of the Garrick memorabilia produced during his lifetime, testimony to his fame and popularity.

Creamware is the term used for fine lead-glazed ware with a light coloured body which was developed and manufactured by Josiah Wedgwood, and also at the Staffordshire and Leeds factories from the 1760s. Creamware was not used for dining on the grandest scale but was rather intended for the middle classes, and it was often more decorative than purely functional. RB

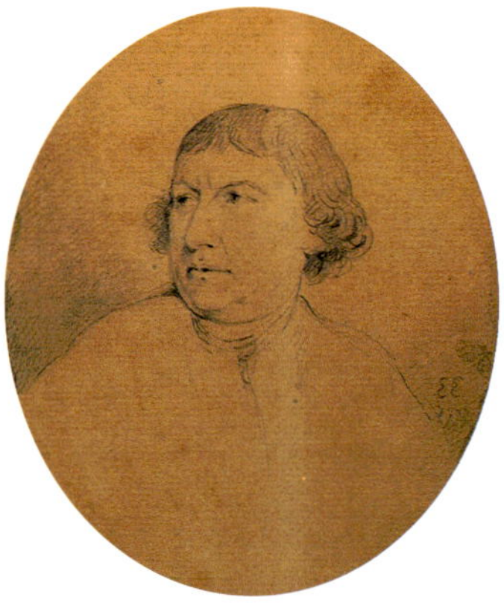

46 **Edward Edwards**
David Garrick
Victoria and Albert Museum.

46 Edward Edwards (1738–1806)

***David Garrick*, 1777**

Pencil on paper, 57.5 × 42.3 cm

Victoria and Albert Museum

Garrick had retired from the stage and from the management of the Theatre Royal the year before this drawing was made, suffering from ill-health and exhaustion. This drawing is thought to be the last portrait of him from life, and his furrowed brow and aged appearance are indicative of what had been a particularly stressful final season. His last performance was as Don Felix in *The Wonder*, after which Garrick gave an emotional farewell speech:

> This is to me a very awful moment; it is no less than parting for ever with those from whom I have received the greatest kindness and favours, and upon the spot where that kindness and those favours were enjoyed.

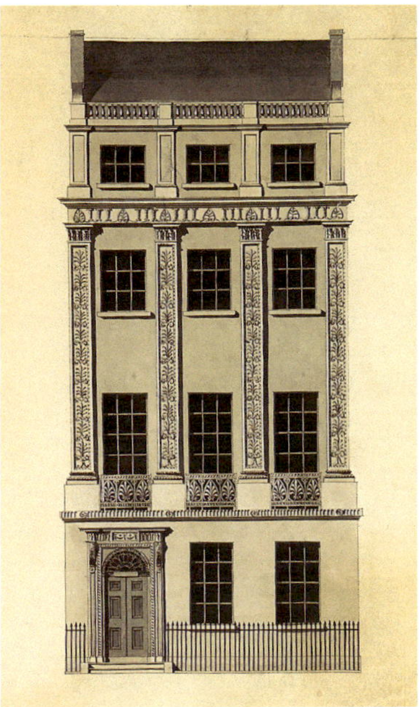

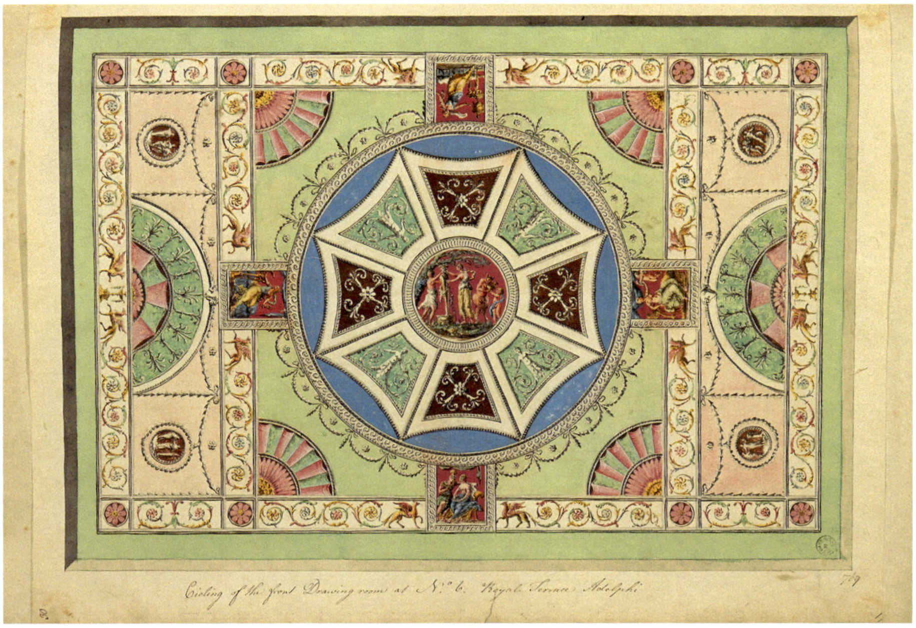

Edwards had recently returned from Italy when he made this drawing. He had been a student at the St. Martin's Lane Academy and, like Van der Gucht (cat. no. 35), was one of the first students to enrol in the Royal Academy Schools. RB

(above left)

47 Robert Adam
Elevation
Sir John Soane's Museum.

(above)

48 Robert Adam
Drawing room ceiling
Sir John Soane's Museum.

Robert Adam (1728–1792)

47 **Elevation of a House for David Garrick Esq.,** 1771
Pen, ink & wash, 57 × 38 cm
Trustees of Sir John Soane's Museum *(Adam vol. 42/60)*

48 **Ceiling of the Grand Drawing Room,** 1771
Pen, ink, watercolour and bodycolour, 44 × 59 cm
Trustees of Sir John Soane's Museum *(Adam vol. 13/30)*

49 **Ceiling of the Back Drawing Room,** 1771
Pen, ink, watercolour and bodycolour, 65 × 51 cm
Trustees of Sir John Soane's Museum *(Adam vol. 13/31)*

In 1772, after twenty years in Southampton Row, David Garrick moved to No. 5 Royal Terrace, the central house in a development on the Thames designed by Robert Adam and named 'The Adelphi'. He was the first resident, and he died there. On 30 April 1772 Fanny Burney described her visit: '...we were so happy as to be let in at Mr Garrick's, and saw his new house in the Adelphi buildings, a sweet situation. The house is large and most elegantly fitted up.'

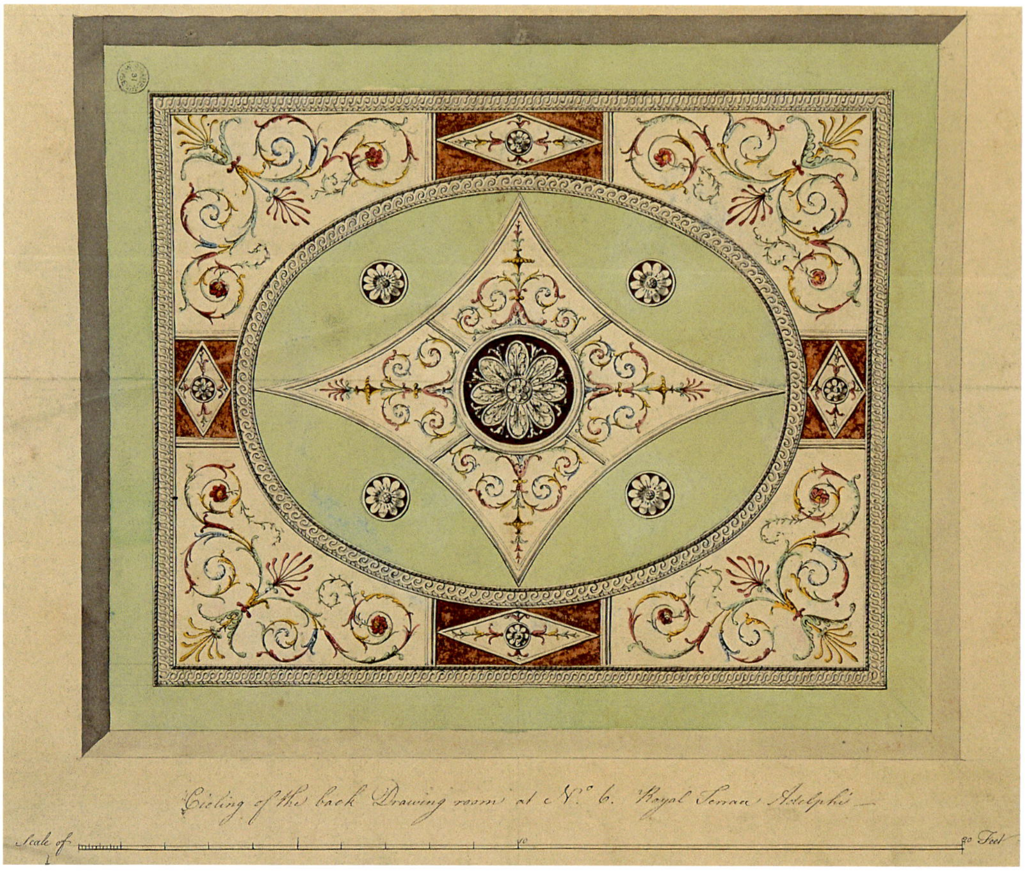

49 Robert Adam
Ceiling of the back drawing room
Sir John Soane's Museum.

No. 5 was furnished by Thomas Chippendale (1717–1779), and bills of £931 9*s*. 3*d*. were accumulated between January 1771 and April 1772. The Adelphi was demolished in the 1930s but the ceiling of Garrick's Drawing Room was presented to the Victoria & Albert Museum, where it is displayed in the new British Galleries.

The history of the Adelphi has been narrated elsewhere, notably by Arthur Bolton in *The Architecture of Robert and James Adam* (Country Life, 1922). By the late 1760s Robert Adam was the most fashionable architect in Britain, and with two of his brothers operated a building firm with several hundred employees. However, he had not yet realised his vision of a building in London that prominently displayed the classical magnificence of which he had dreamed in his years as a student in Rome. The Adelphi – the word is Greek for 'brothers' – was their opportunity. The facades of the two central houses in Royal Terrace were decorated with stucco pilasters enriched with the light neo-classical ornaments typical of the architect's style. Below was a vaulted basement whose monumentality recalled Roman engineering.

Its construction was opposed by the City of London in a petition received by Parliament in May 1771, and the following month the *Town and Country Magazine* published a 'puff' for the Adams' project, in which Garrick was the only resident to be identified: 'one of the centre houses is purchased by Mr Garrick, and is almost completely fitted up in a truly classic style'.

A celebrated resident who would open his doors to society was a critical element in Adam's project to create a wealthy neighbourhood in an unfashionable area, standing between the squalor of the Strand and the mud of the Thames. Adam chose to live next door to Garrick, and his house and its furnishings would have presented his own abilities to clients. An exquisite clock, mirror and girandole were reproduced in the brothers' *Works in Architecture* (1773). At the same time he was negotiating with Matthew Boulton and the silversmith Cox to open shops in the development.

Adam had remodelled Garrick's villa at Hampton in 1765 and rebuilt the Drury Lane Theatre. They had become friends, and Garrick jokingly addressed the brothers as 'those unprincipled Gentlemen, and vile architects the Adams'. At Drury Lane the pilasters were decorated with plate-glass from the British Plate-Glass manufactory at St Helen's in Lancashire, in which Garrick had invested. It is evident that each man understood the value of mutual publicity. By 1773 the Adams were in financial trouble, and to rescue the project they initiated a Lottery in which the prizes were houses in The Adelphi.

Whatever his importance to the prestige of The Adelphi, Garrick seems to have enjoyed his 'sweet situation', placing a telescope to survey the Thames from the Library on the ground floor, a room in which he also displayed Hogarth's *Satan, Sin and Death* (cat. no. 53) and drawings including the portrait by Nathaniel Dance (cat. no. 39).

The first-floor drawing rooms of Royal Terrace were decorated with ornamental plaster ceilings; as the *Town and Country* magazine noted,

> The ceiling of the front room on the principal floor is painted by [Antonio] Zucchi, in the middle of which [are] represented the Graces attiring Venus, Cupid standing by her. The chimneypiece in the apartment is of white marble, finely sculptured, and is said to have cost three hundred pounds.

This Room was hung with Old Masters, but the Dining Room at the rear of the ground floor was a set-piece celebrating Garrick. Zoffany's paintings of Garrick in tragic and comic roles (cat. no.s 19 and 14) were placed opposite the fireplace, facing those of the villa at Hampton (cat. no.s 16 and 17) on the opposite wall. Over the doors were a second scene of Hampton (cat. no. 18) and a portrait of Garrick's brother George's two daughters playing in the gardens. CW

50 Sketch plan and elevation of a garden seat for Hampton

Pencil, 20.5 × 20.5 cm

The Trustees of Sir John Soane's Museum *(Adam vol. 21/125)*

INSCRIBED *Mrs Garrick wishes to have a small seat for the lawn beside the house at Hampton Court, could not one be made with the whole basement cast of Liardet to put upon a [?Wall].*

In 1755 David Garrick bought a villa by the Thames at Hampton as a place to retreat to from the pressures of the West End and to entertain friends, as described in Letitia Galbraith's article in *Apollo*, July 1972. He remodelled the house on its purchase and commissioned Robert Adam to make a series of improvements in the years which followed.

Although the Temple to Shakespeare built in 1755 was not designed by Robert Adam, he did design a number of structures to ornament the garden, landscaped in the natural style of 'Capability' Brown.

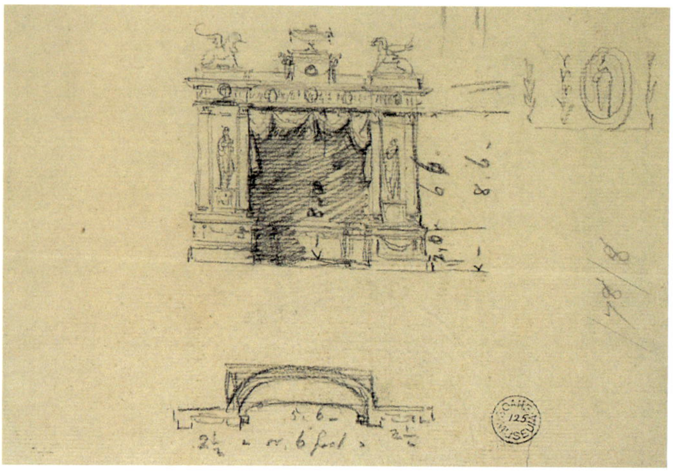

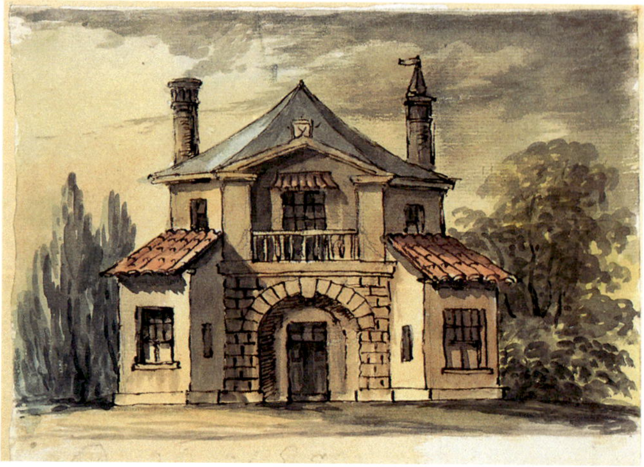

(above)
50 Robert Adam
Garden seat
Sir John Soane's Museum.

(above right)
51 Robert Adam
Design for a Lodge
Sir John Soane's Museum.

This design is a response to Mrs Garrick's wish for a garden seat beside the lawn. Adam imagined his friends David and Eva sitting side by side (as in cat. no. 42 perhaps) in an alcove framed by stage curtains. Six feet in length and eleven feet in height, it was decorated in an ornate neo-classical style and with two figures which may represent Comedy and Tragedy. This combination of theatre design and garden architecture is unique in Adam's oeuvre, and is a further instance of Garrick's ability to lead artists' imaginations in new directions. It was never built.

CW

51 Design for a Lodge, 1777
Pen and coloured washes, 17 × 20 cm
The Trustees of Sir John Soane's Museum *(Adam vol. 2/137)*
INSCRIBED *David Garrick Esq.*, 1777

This drawing is only identified with Garrick by the inscription and no location is indicated. It is typical of hundreds of designs made by Adam for ornamental 'fantasies' in a variety of styles. Few were actual commissions; they were opportunities for the architect to exercise his imagination and to explore the possibilities of Picturesque composition. This design combines a number of 'rustic' elements to form a structure which has many similarities to the ornamental hermitages popular at this period.

In 1776 Garrick had sold the Drury Lane Theatre and was airing his ideas for retirement to his friends. It is possible that the design is the architect's response to his friend's yearning for quietness and solitude.

CW

52 William Hogarth (1697–1764)
***The Wedding Banquet**, c. 1745*
Oil on canvas, 71 × 93 cm
Royal Cornwall Museum

The Wedding Banquet was intended as number three in *The Happy Marriage* series, originally planned as a rustic companion to *Marriage A-la-Mode* (National Gallery), but the series was never completed. This scene shows the ceremony of breaking the cake over the heads of the bride and groom. Garrick hung this painting in the dining room at Hampton. Hogarth's series *Marriage A-la-Mode* inspired Garrick and his friend George Colman to collaborate in writing

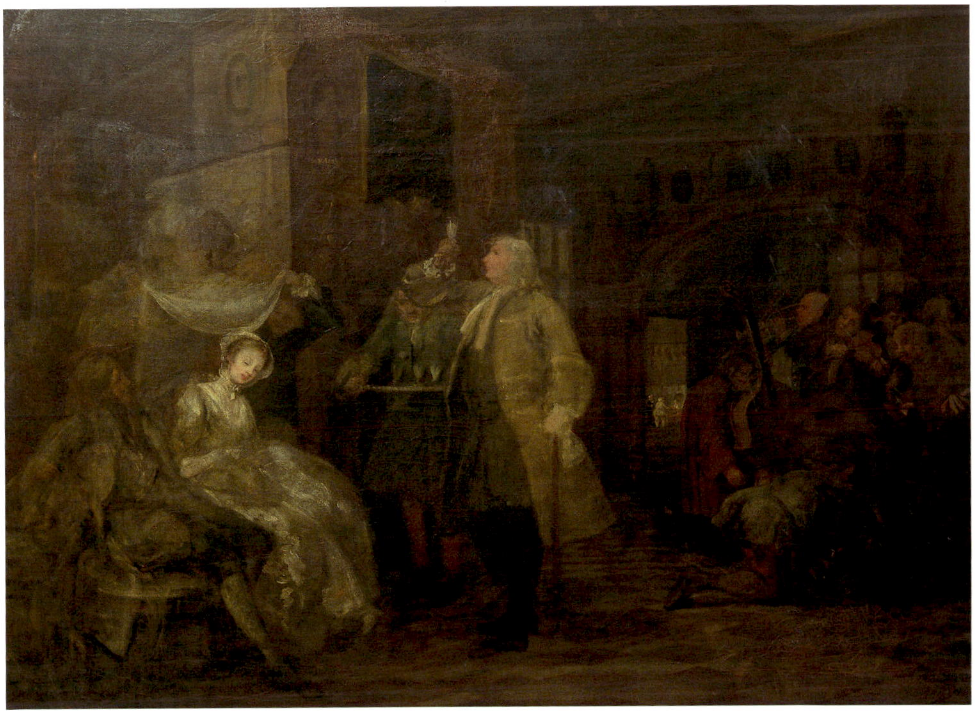

52 **William Hogarth**
The Wedding Banquet
Royal Cornwall Museum.

the play *The Clandestine Marriage*, which opened in February 1766, and in which they paid tribute to the artist:

> Tonight your matchless Hogarth gives the thought,
> Which from his canvas to the stage is brought

George Steevens, who frequently studied in Garrick's library, recounts in his *Anecdotes* of 1781 how Hogarth was so delighted with this painting that on completion he carried it to Garrick 'in triumph'. However, if Hogarth had intended to finish the series, and have it engraved, it seems unlikely that he would part with the painting in such a way.

According to Hogarth's friend, the artist Benjamin Wilson, the head of the bride was painted shortly before Hogarth's death and was modelled on Queen Charlotte; this implies that the picture was not in Garrick's collection until after 1764, possibly acquired with *Satan, Sin and Death* (cat. no. 53). It is described in Garrick's inventory as being 'a sketch'. The painting was greatly admired by George III, who borrowed it from Garrick in 1776 and thought the bride 'a handsome likeness of the Queen'.[42] RB

53 William Hogarth (1697–1764)

***Satan, Sin and Death**, c. 1735–40*
Oil on canvas, 61.9 × 74.5cm
Tate

Satan, Sin and Death illustrates a scene from John Milton's *Paradise Lost*. In 1734 Jonathan Richardson published *Explanatory notes on Paradise Lost*, a commentary in which he identified this scene, the end of Book II, as being key to the whole work. He discussed his work at the

42. Ronald Paulson, *Hogarth: His Life, Art, and Times*, London 1971, pp. 18–19.

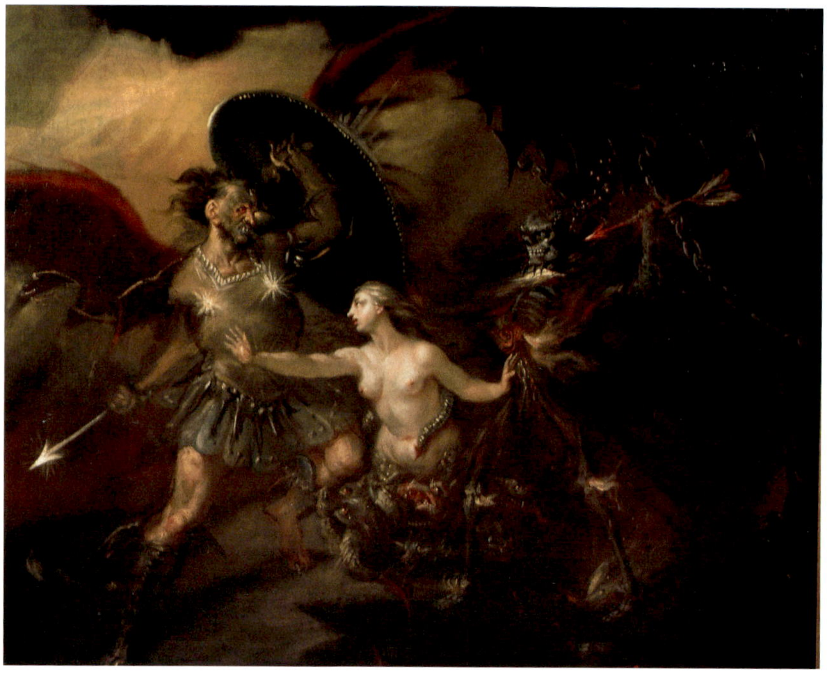

53 **William Hogarth**
Satan, Sin and Death
Tate.

literary club attended by Hogarth at Slaughter's Coffee House. The style of the painting suggests that *Satan, Sin and Death* was painted at this time, but that it was abandoned for formal reasons; Satan's right arm has been rubbed out and redrawn in outline, but not resolved.[43] Hogarth may have returned to the work in 1757 when Edmund Burke's *Philosophical Enquiry into... the Sublime and Beautiful* singled out the description of Death as an example of the purest sublimity, and he challenged painting to meet poetry in such an achievement.

Satan, Sin and Death hung in Garrick's library in London from 1772, when Garrick moved to the Adelphi Terrace. It was not commissioned by Garrick, whom Hogarth did not meet until the early 1740s. A lost engraving by Townley, made in 1767, records the painting as being in Garrick's collection, unfinished. It had probably remained in Hogarth's studio as an unresolved piece of work until the artist's death, when it was acquired by Garrick along with *The Wedding Banquet* (cat. no. 52). It was a curious addition to Garrick's large collection, the majority of which is portraiture and landscape; literary illustrations are limited to scenes from Shakespeare, including two versions of *Falstaff enlisting his Recruits*, one by Hogarth, the other by Hayman. It is likely that Garrick saw this painting in Hogarth's studio, and the two may have discussed its progress. Garrick was an admirer of Milton, and he owned a portrait of the poet, listed in his inventory as by Jeremy Andrews, and which hung in the green drawing room at Hampton.

Garrick had, some years before acquiring this painting, been asked to give an opinion on how to represent scenes from *Paradise Lost*. In a letter to Francis Hayman of 1745, he refers to the illustrations to Dr Thomas Newton's edition of Milton, on which Hayman was working: 'Your drawings for Milton will do you great Service, I have promis'd the Doctor to read Y^{e} third book and give him my opinion for the Drawing, wch I will send you.' Hayman's drawing of *Satan, Sin and Death*, engraved by Grignion, was the frontispiece to Book II, and was published in 1749.

43. David Bindman, 'Hogarth's *Satan, Sin and Death* and its influence', *Burlington Magazine*, no. 112, 1970, pp. 153–158.

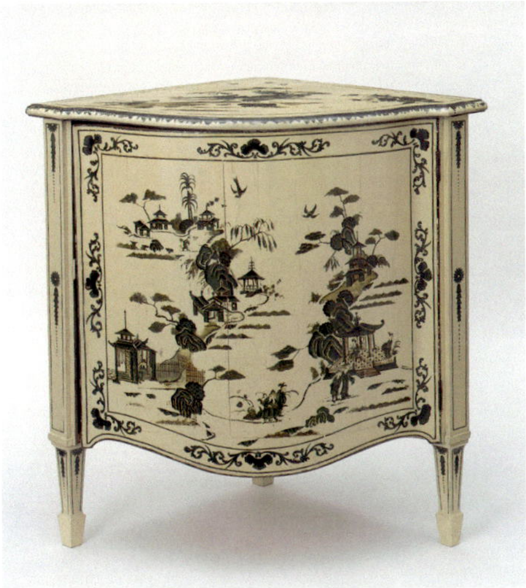
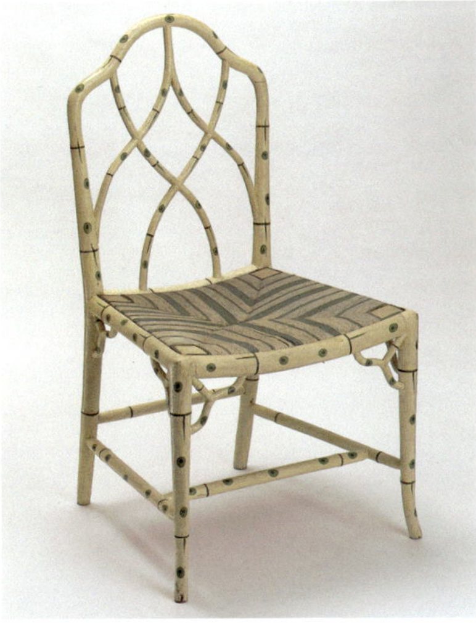
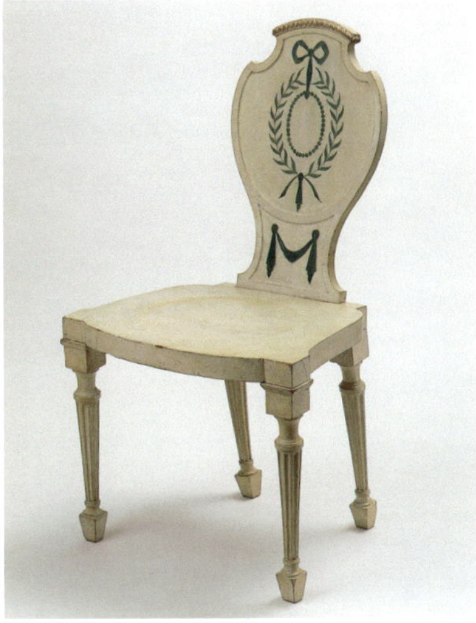

(above left)
54 Thomas Chippendale
Corner cabinet
Victoria and Albert Museum.

(above middle)
56 Thomas Chippendale
Rush seated chair
Victoria and Albert Museum.

(above right)
55 Thomas Chippendale
Hall Chair
Victoria and Albert Museum.

Satan, Sin and Death is an insight into Garrick and Hogarth's shared ambitions for the visual arts. Hogarth aspired to paint history pictures in the 'Grand Manner' as well as the comic scenes for which he had become famous, and Garrick was keen to demonstrate that he could excel in both tragic and comic roles. RB

Thomas Chippendale (1718–1779)

54 **Corner cabinet, W24.1917,** *c.*1770
96.5 cm high

55 **Hall chair, W32.1937,** *c.*1775
98cm high

56 **Two rush-seated chairs W27.1917 and W28.1917,** *c.*1770
91.5 cm high

57 **Towel horse, W32. 1917,** *c.*1770
93 cm high
Beech, birch and pine, painted green and white and varnished
Victoria and Albert Museum

David and Eva Garrick acquired the villa at Hampton in 1754. They furnished and improved it gradually over twenty years, in a light and informal style that was entirely appropriate to its role as a country retreat for themselves and their friends. A commentator in 1768 remarked that:

> In the house neither magnificence or fashion are to be discovered; but instead of these a pleasing, noble simplicity, which seems to belong to a country life.

Many of the rooms were decorated in a fashionable pseudo-oriental or 'Chinoiserie' style.

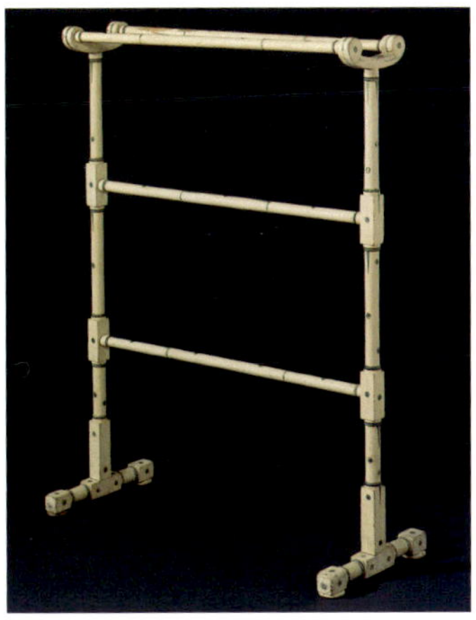

(above)
57 Thomas Chippendale
Towel Horse
Victoria and Albert Museum.

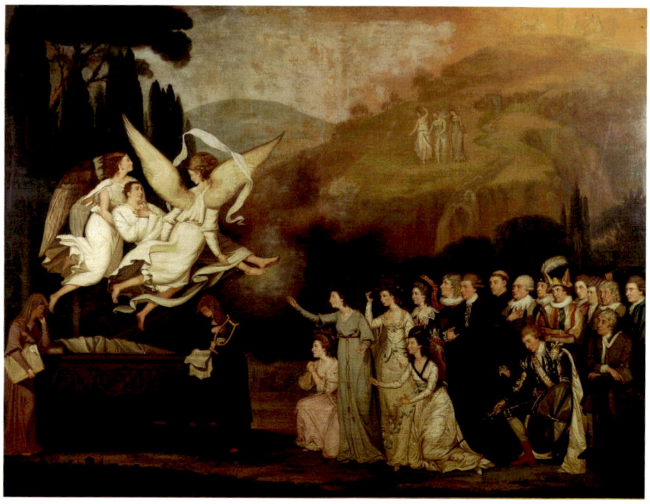

58 **George Carter**
The Apotheosis of Garrick
Royal Shakespeare Company Collection.

The decorative designer and decorator Jean Pillement (1728–1808) provided Chinoiserie panels for the first-floor Drawing Room in 1757. The renowned cabinet-maker Thomas Chippendale equipped the house between *c.* 1768 and *c.* 1775 with delicate and fanciful furniture which contrasted with the more formal furniture he provided for the Garricks' town house in the Adelphi Terrace.

The corner commode was provided as part of the suite of green and white japanned furniture for the Garricks' own bedchamber and dressing room, which was hung with Chinese wall-paper and Indian Chintz. The hall chair is one of an original set of four supplied in *c.* 1775, and is decorated in a slightly more formal, classical style befitting the entrance to the house. The two rush-seated chairs may be those recorded as part of a set of six in the first-floor Chinese Drawing Room in the inventory of the house taken in 1779, although Mrs. Garrick continued to order simple rush-seated chairs by other manufacturers for the house during her long widowhood. Their original painted and varnished surfaces have been repaired and renewed. The towel rail or 'horse' was probably supplied in 1768. Beneath the current green and white decoration are traces of earlier blue and white paint, which may indicate that this piece was part of the blue and white japanned suite of furniture provided for the guest bedchamber on the first floor of the villa. LW

58 George Carter (1737–1794)
The Apotheosis of Garrick, 1780
Oil on canvas, 141 × 196.8 cm
Royal Shakespeare Company Collection, Stratford upon Avon

Mr. Carter having finished his picture to the memory of the late Mr. Garrick, begs most respectfully to acquaint his numerous subscribers, and the admirers at large of that great character, that the picture is now open … for their inspection, at his house in Margaret street,

> Cavendish Square, Every Day, where Subscriptions are taken in for the print ... NB There are in this work Seventeen portraits of the principle performers, besides that of Mr. Garrick.[44]

It is evident from this advertisement that Carter was keen to capitalize on Garrick's memory and the spectacle of his lying-in and funeral, attended by many of the actors Carter has represented in this painting. They appear here in Shakespearian roles, including Mrs Abingdon as Beatrice, raising a mask from her eyes, Mr King as Touchstone in his striped costume and Mrs Yates as Isabella, kneeling with hands clasped. He published a key to these figures to accompany prints of the picture. The painting was shown at the Royal Academy in 1784 when Horace Walpole described it as 'Ridiculous and Bad'. George Carter was initially self-taught, entering the Royal Academy schools in 1770. In 1785 he held a private exhibition of thirty-five history pictures, accompanied by a large catalogue. The following year he left for Calcutta, where he painted scenes from Indian history.

59 R. Evan Sly

Garrick and Hogarth or the Artist Puzzled, 1845
Coloured lithograph, 28 × 37 cm
Trustees of the British Museum
INSCRIBED *No.5 of R Evan Sly's new & amusing mechanical Prints / Garrick and Hogarth or the Artist Puzzled / Designed and drawn on stone by R. Evan Sly / While Garrick sat for Hogarth for his own picture he mischievously altered his countenance so as to render the portrait perfectly unlike. Hogarth blamed the unlucky effort on his art and began a second time but with the same success; after swearing a little he began a third time and did not discover the trick until after many repetitions. He then got into a violent passion and would have thrown his pallet and brushes at Garrick's head if the wag had not made his escape from the storm of variegated colours. This print contains a correct profile of Hogarth and 30 different likenesses of David Garrick from pictures by Sir J. Reynolds, Gainsborough, Parkinson, Roberts and etc., also 30 sketches of Heads selected from Hogarth's best pictures.*

The rotating disc behind this print shows thirty different likenesses of Garrick, as described in the inscription, first recounted in the *London Chronicle* in November 1786.[45] Different images also appear for the sketch lying on the floor. Garrick's face was famously mobile and expressive. Dr Johnson commented:

> I don't believe he kept the same look for half-an-hour together in the whole of his life; and such an eternal, restless, fatiguing play of muscles must certainly wear out a man's face before its time.

For this print, Evan Sly has made use of the popular conception that artists found Garrick's expressive face extremely difficult to paint. When painting Garrick as Richard III (fig. 1), Hogarth found the face so difficult that he eventually painted it on a separate piece of canvas and attached it to the portrait. Evan Sly may also be alluding to the quarrel Hogarth and Garrick are said to have had over the portrait of *Garrick and his Wife* (fig. 4). Garrick did not

44. Quoted in Shearer West, *The Image of the Actor*, London 1991, p. 37.

45. Jenny Uglow, *Hogarth, a Life and a World*, London 1997, p. 589.

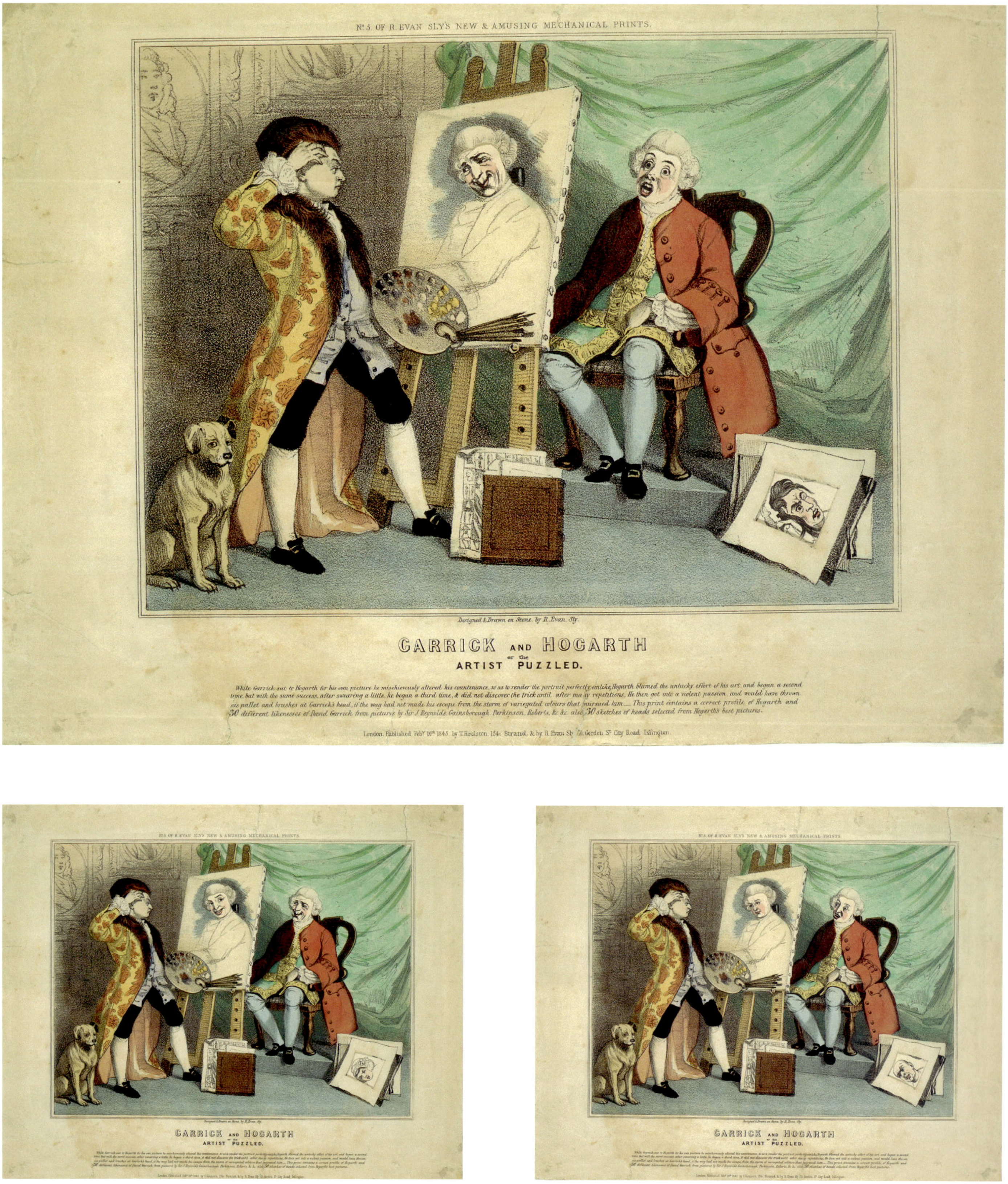

59 R. Evan Sly, *Garrick and Hogarth or The Artist Puzzled*
Trustees of the British Museum.

like the expression Hogarth had depicted. Hogarth, in frustration, temporarily blacked out the face and kept the portrait in his studio until he died, when his widow gave it to Mrs Garrick, possibly after Garrick's death, and she hung it above the fireplace in the dining room at the Adelphi.

Gainsborough's obituary in *The Morning Chronicle*, August 1788, reveals that he suffered similar difficulties when painting Garrick (see p.14). The print, with its thirty different likeness, also serves to demonstrate that the great portraits of Garrick were remarkable because of the sheer number executed. RB

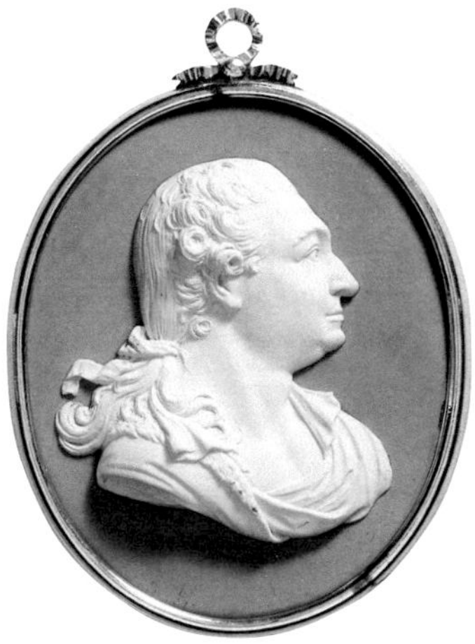

60 **Wedgwood**
David Garrick
Trustees of the British Museum.

60 Wedgwood and Bentley, modelled by William Hackwood (*c.* 1757–1839)

David Garrick, 1777–80
Grey-blue jasper, 10.5 cm high
Trustees of the British Museum

This medallion was modelled after a medal by Lewis Pingo of 1772, which compares to the drawing by John Keyse Sherwin of about the same time (cat. no. 41), and the subsequent engraving of 1774. This is another example of the Classicising profile portrait associated with eternal fame that was considered appropriate for depictions of Garrick in the 1770s. This medallion was produced in conjunction with a similar medallion of Shakespeare, a pairing which demonstrates the enduring association of Garrick and Shakespeare in the eyes of Garrick's contemporaries. RB

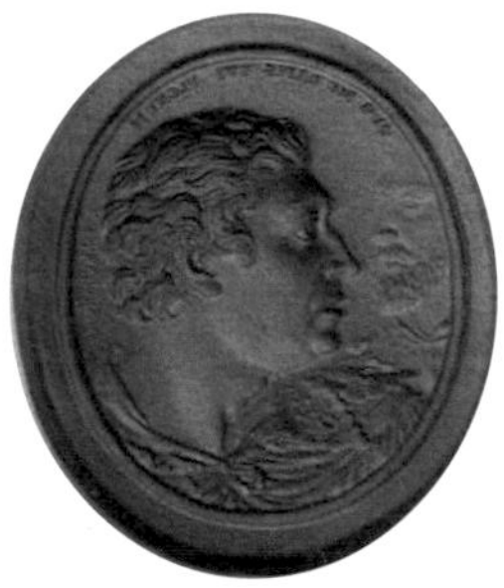

61 **Wedgwood**
David Garrick looking into the face of Shakespeare
The Holburne Museum of Art.

61 Wedgwood and Bentley after Nathaniel Marchant (1739–1816)

Intaglio showing David Garrick looking into the face of Shakespeare, late eighteenth century
Black basalt, 2 cm high
The Holburne Museum of Art
INSCRIBED *Quo Me Rapis Tui Plenum*
SIGNED *MARCHANTF*

This intaglio shows David Garrick on its obverse side, looking in the face of his hero Shakespeare. The legend can be translated as, 'Where are you carrying me away to, filled with your spirit?'[46] It illustrates the concept of 'genius' that Gainsborough had grappled with when painting Garrick in 1766 (cat. no.s 33 and 34), and when attempting to paint a portrait of Shakespeare. The reverse of the intaglio shows a bust of Cleopatra, facing to the right. Nathaniel Marchant was an admired gem-cutter and medallist. RB

62 Bow porcelain factory

***Henry Woodward as The Fine Gentleman in Garrick's 'Lethe'**, c. 1750*
Soft-paste porcelain, glazed, 29.2 cm high
The Holburne Museum of Art

The Fine Gentleman is one of the ten characters who each deliver a humorous monologue in Garrick's farce *Lethe: or Aesop in the Shades*, first performed at Drury Lane in 1740, before he

46. Suggested in Aileen Dawson, *British Museum Masterpieces of Wedgwood*, London 1984, p. 36.

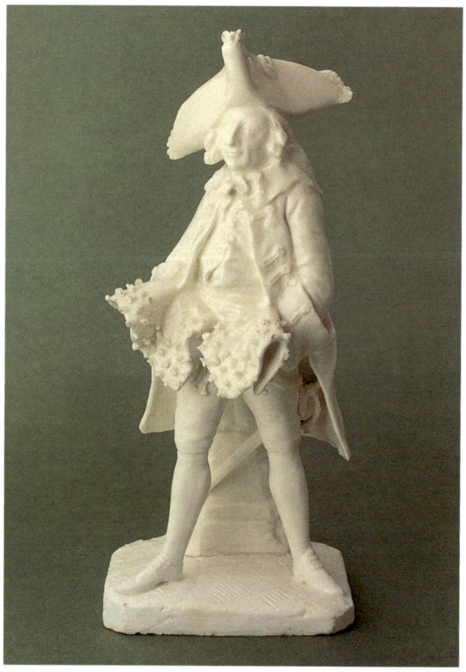

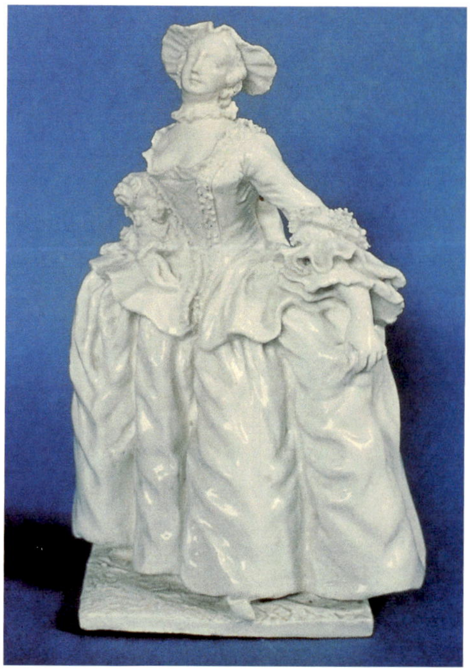

(right)
62 Bow porcelain factory
Henry Woodward as The Fine Gentleman
The Holburne Museum of Art.

(far right)
63 Bow porcelain factory
Kitty Clive as The Fine Lady
The Holburne Museum of Art.

had made his own acting debut. The Fine Gentleman is intended to satirise the behaviour of some wealthy gentleman theatre-goers, particularly those who were tempted to participate in the on-stage action:

> I dress in the evening and go generally behind the scenes of both playhouses; not, you may imagine, to be diverted with the play, but to intrigue and show myself. I stand upon the stage, talk loud and stare about, which confounds the actors and disturbs the audience. Upon the galleries, who hate the appearance of one of us, begin to hiss and cry 'Off, off!' while I undaunted stamp my foot so, loll with my shoulder thus, take snuff with my right hand and smile scornfully, thus. This exasperates the savages, and they attack us with vollies of sucked oranges and half-eaten pippins.

Henry Woodward (1714–1777) was in the first performance, and in many subsequent productions. This figure was inspired by a mezzotint by James McArdell published in 1750, after a drawing by Hayman (Fitzwilliam Museum, Cambridge). It has a pair, (cat. no. 63) depicting Kitty Clive as The Fine Lady. RB

63 Bow porcelain factory
***Kitty Clive as The Fine Lady in Garrick's 'Lethe'**, c. 1750*
Soft-paste porcelain, glazed, 24.4 cm high
The Holburne Museum of Art

This figure of Kitty Clive as The Fine Lady is the pair to Henry Woodward as The Fine Gentleman (cat. no. 62). Garrick's description of The Fine Lady in *Lethe* reveals her to be shallow and frivolous:

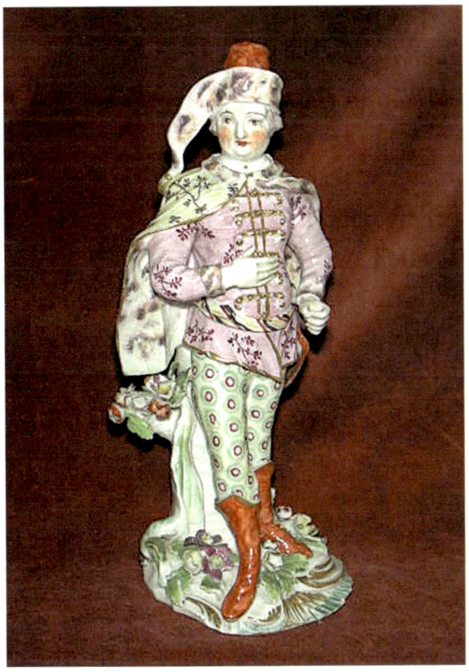

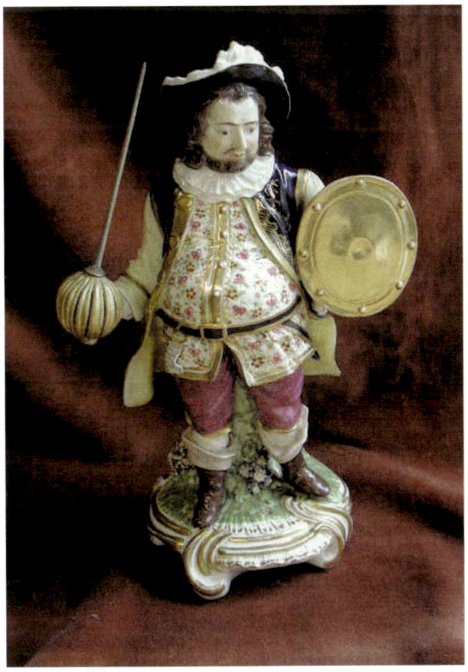

(far left)
64 **Chelsea porcelain factory**
David Garrick as Tancred
The Holburne Museum of Art.

(left)
66 **Derby porcelain factory**
James Quin as Falstaff
The Holburne Museum of Art.

> She lies in bed all morning, rattles about all day; sits up all night, she goes everywhere and sees everything, knows everyone and loves nobody; ridicules her friends, coquettes with her lovers, sets them together by their ears, tells fibs, makes mischief, buys china, cheats at cards, keeps a pet dog and hates parsons.

Catherine (Kitty) Clive (1711-1785) was a popular comic actress who worked under Garrick's management at Drury Lane from 1746 until her retirement in 1769. Although Clive was often jealous and demanding, she and Garrick remained respectful of each other's talent and popularity. This figure was modelled from an engraving by Charles Mosley, published in 1750. RB

64 Chelsea porcelain factory

David Garrick as Tancred, 1760
Soft-paste porcelain, decorated in enamel colours with gilding, glazed, 22 cm high
The Holburne Museum of Art

Garrick is shown wearing the exotic costume of the hero Tancred in James Thomson's 1745 drama *Tancred and Sigismunda*. Tancred is the twelfth-century heir to the throne of Sicily, doomed in his love for Sigismunda. Although Walpole described the play as 'very dull', it proved popular and featured in eighteen seasons at Drury Lane. The costume Garrick wore during this production was not historically accurate, but was rather based on the uniform of the Hungarian Hussars, who were fighting at the time in the War of the Austrian Succession. When compared to the portrait of Garrick in this role by Thomas Worlidge (Garrick Club), it seems evident that the Chelsea porcelain factory has elaborated on this costume even further. This is a pair to the figure showing Mrs Cibber as Sigismunda. RB

65 Chelsea Porcelain factory

Mrs Cibber as Sigismunda in 'Tancred and Sigismunda', c. 1760
Soft-paste porcelain, decorated in enamel colours with gilding, glazed, 22 cm high
The Holburne Museum of Art

This figure is the unmatched pair to *Garrick as Tancred* (cat. no. 64). Susanna Cibber (1714–1766) had a low-pitched voice and a sad cast to her eyes, and was considered very affecting in tragic roles, such as Sigismunda. The tale of the ill-fated lovers, Tancred and Sigismunda, concludes tragically, when they both die at the hands of Osmond, Sigismunda's spurned husband. Garrick and Mrs Cibber endured a similarly painful finale when acting together in Otway's *Venice Preserv'd* (cat. no. 19).

Mrs Cibber began her stage career in 1732, as a singer. She was a favourite of Handel, singing the contralto arias in the first performance of *Messiah* in 1742. Garrick first cast Mrs Cibber as his leading lady in Shakespeare's *King John* in 1742, persuaded, it would seem, by the actor Thomas Quin, who exclaimed: 'That woman has a heart, and can do anything where passion is required!'. They were considered to be a well-matched stage partnership:

> From similarity of complexion, size, and countenance, they could have been easily supposed to be brother and sister; but in the powerful expression of the passions, they still approached to a near resemblance.[47]

RB

66 Derby porcelain factory

James Quin as Falstaff, c. 1765
Soft-paste porcelain, decorated in enamel colours with gilding, glazed, 29.6 cm high
The Holburne Museum of Art

The character of Falstaff from *Henry IV, part 1* was one of James Quin's most famous roles. His build and temperament meant that he was well suited for the part . Despite the famous rivalry between the two actors, Quin and Garrick worked together amicably at Covent Garden during the 1740s. Garrick played Hotspur to Quin's Falstaff in 1746, where their physical dissimilarities were put to good effect (see cat. no. 5):

> Quin had little or no difficulty in perching Garrick upon his shoulders, who looked like a dwarf on the back of a giant.[48]

This figure is modelled after a mezzotint engraving by James McArdell, distributed in 1751. It was a popular print and continued to sell until the end of the century. This figure is by the Derby factory, which manufactured the figure in six different sizes to meet public demand. Figures of Quin, based on the same mezzotint, were also produced by the Bow manufactory and in the Staffordshire potteries. Garrick, who particularly admired Quin's performance as Falstaff, owned one of the Derby figures, and also owned two portraits of Quin as *Falstaff reviewing the Recruits*, by Hogarth and by Hayman.

RB

47. Thomas Davies, *Memoirs of a Life of David Garrick*, 2 vols., London 1808, I, pp. 116–117.

48. Thomas Davies, *Dramatic Miscellanies*, 3 vols., London 1784, I, p. 274.

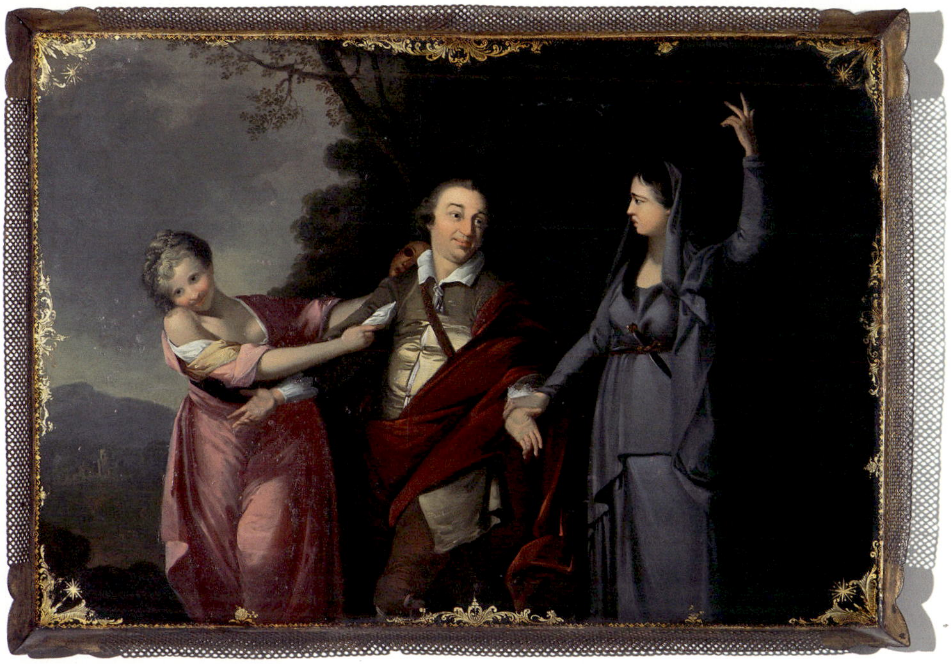

68 Pontypool Tray decorated with Reynolds's *Garrick between Tragedy and Comedy*
Private collection.

67 William Vincent (*c.*1740–1793)

Tea Casket containing Three Tea Caddies, 1771–2

Silver cage-work over shagreen-covered wooden base, lined red velvet; blue glass caddies, 23 cm high

Bristol City Museum and Art Gallery

MARKS (under one caddy) lion passant, leopard's head, date letter 'Q', maker's mark WV for William Vincent.

The decorations on this tea casket are taken from London theatrical engravings published between 1765 and 1777. They feature several actors contemporary with Garrick, but Garrick is the most dominant figure. The long side of the tea chest, on the left-hand side, shows Garrick as Tancred in Act IV, scene II, of James Thomson's *Tancred and Sigismunda*, a reversed impression of the engraving by Collyer after Isaac Taylor. The right-hand side shows Garrick as Sir John Brute in Act III, scene I of Vanbrugh's *The Provok'd Wife* (cat. no. 22). The ends of the casket show Mrs Abington as Lady Betty Modish in Colley Cibber's *The Careless Husband* and Garrick as Don Jon in Act I, scene III of Beaumont and Fletcher's *The Chances*, after de Loutherbourg (cat. no. 44).

The illustrations depicted on two of the tea caddies, inside the casket, have not been identified. Identifications of illustrations have been made for the third caddy, the sides of which show Charles Dibdin as Mungo in Isaac Bickerstaffe's *The Padlock,* Samuel Foote as The Doctor in his own play *The Devil upon Two Sticks,* and Charles Macklin as Shylock in Act IV, scene II of *The Merchant of Venice*. The final side shows Garrick as Lord Chalkstone in his own play *Lethe*, taken from a print by John Smith after Zoffany's painting (Garrick Club). RB

68 Pontypool Factory after Sir Joshua Reynolds (1723–1792)
Tray decorated with 'Garrick between Tragedy and Comedy', *1770–90s*
Japanned tinplate, 55 × 75 cm
Private collection

The tray is decorated with Reynolds's painting of *Garrick between Tragedy and Comedy* (cat. no. 11), one of the most popular portraits of the actor. Several copies of the painting were made, as well as the 1762 engraving by Edward Fisher (cat. no. 12).

The celebrated Pontypool japan workshop was founded in 1720 by Edward Allgood. The factory had a reputation for the limited production of superb quality japanning for the nobility and gentry. 'Japanning', decorating a wooden or metal surface with enamel colours, was a term first applied to the decoration of furniture imitating Chinese and Japanese lacquer. Pontypool trays were often decorated with well-known pictures and prints. The artist of the tray is anonymous, but it is very finely painted. The tray was probably made in Wales, and sent to London to be decorated. This tray is another example of expensive and high quality Garrick memorabilia.

RB

69 David Garrick's Dressing Table, 1750s
Pine, 96.5 cm high
The Museum of London

A simple, country-made piece of furniture, in a rather archaic style. The inscription on the silver plate, attached to the dressing table, reads:

> This Dressing Table used by David Garrick at the Theatre Royal Drury Lane, was given by him to John Moody, Actor, by whom it was bequeathed to Edward Layton Esq, Mount Clements, Bushey Heath, Herts

This inscription does not authenticate the table as having once been used by Garrick at Drury Lane, but it is an example of how even the most ordinary objects acquired greater resonance when associated with Garrick. The idea that Garrick applied his greasepaint at this table, in preparation for roles such as *King Lear* and *Richard III* is particularly appealing.

There is, in fact, some credence in the story. Garrick engaged John Moody (1727–1812) at Drury Lane in 1758, where he specialised in low, Irish characters. Moody was particularly supportive of Garrick during the 'Half-Price' riots of 1763. Garrick had introduced a new policy, forbidding the practice of half-price admissions after the end of the third act. The public was incensed, tearing up benches and smashing the chandeliers at the theatre. Moody was quick to prevent disaster, apprehending a vandal trying to set fire to the house, and Garrick was immensely grateful. When the Adam brothers had completed their refurbishment of the theatre in 1775, Garrick wrote to Moody, who was acting in Liverpool for the summer: 'Drury Lane Theatre will delight yr Eyes, when you cast them upon the Old Lady'.

The dressing table, with its associations of backstage camaraderie and anticipation of

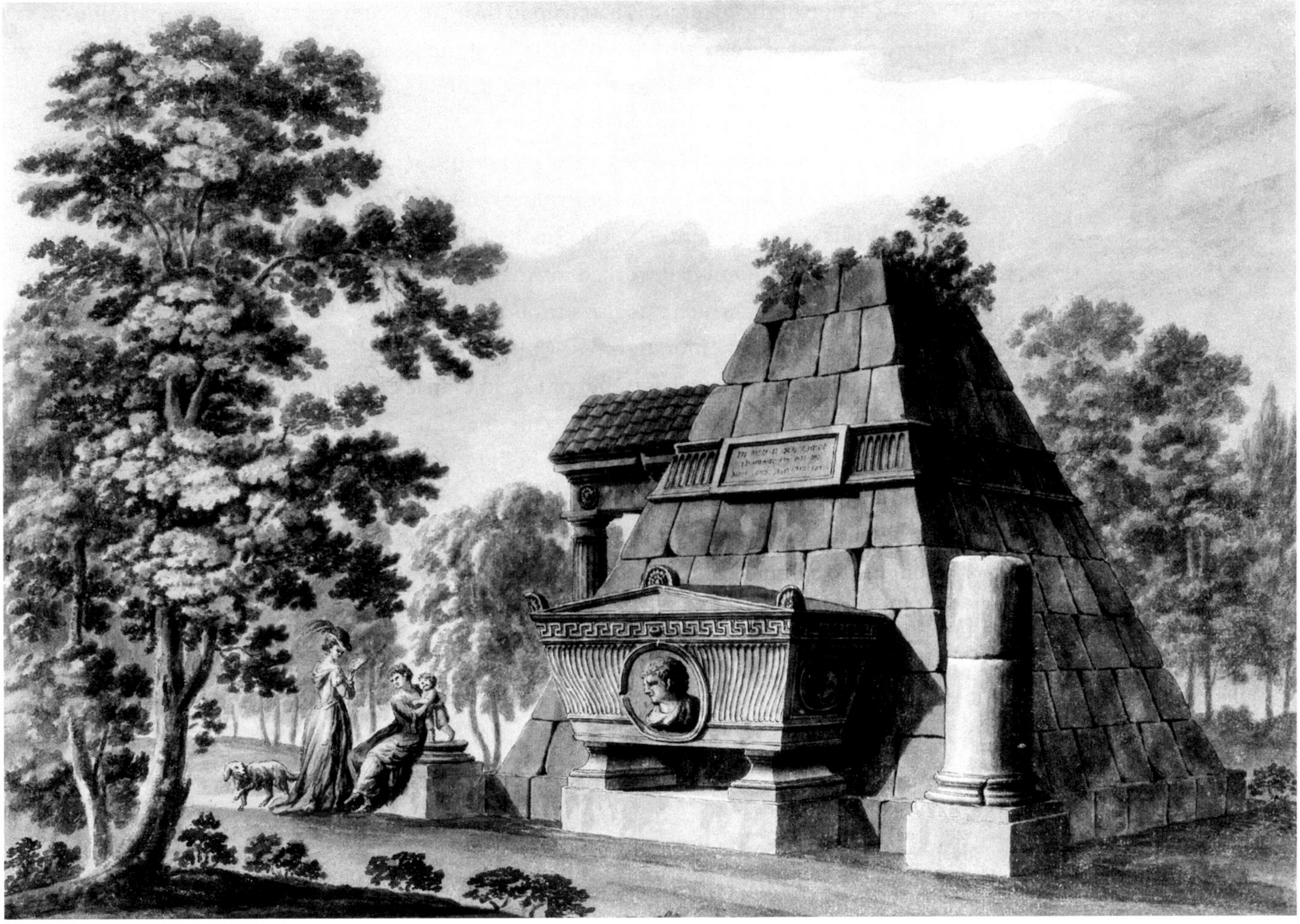

70 **Robert Adam**
Design for Garrick Monument
Trustees of the British Museum.

performance, seems to be an appropriate gift for Moody, a loyal member of the company at Drury Lane, who shared Garrick's great affection for the 'old lady'. RB

70 Robert Adam (1728–1792)

Design for a Cenotaph in memory of David Garrick, 1779

Pen, ink and wash, 42.5 × 57.4.cm

Trustees of the British Museum

Sir Watkin Williams Wynn (1749–1789) was the fabulously rich 'Welsh Maecenas', a patron of art, architecture, theatre, and music. Garrick visited his young admirer's estate at Wynnstay in North Wales in the autumn of 1777, where he supervised an amateur production in the private theatre. Williams Wynn was a pall-bearer at Garrick's funeral and this monument was, no doubt, intended for the park in which his hero had strolled. Preparatory sketches in Sir John Soane's museum made for Sir Watkin suggest that this is the finished perspective of the same design.

The design of the pyramid is based upon the mausoleum of Caius Cestius in Rome, which patron, architect and actor would each have seen and admired on their respective Grand Tours. A pyramid symbolises personal immortality, although Adam's suggestion of its crumbling tip is an allusion to the transience of any individual's achievements. The form was also an important component in Neo-classical composition and this design predates the two most prominent pyramidical mausolea in Britain, built for Lord Darnley at Cobham Hall, Kent by James Wyatt (1782) and for the Earl of Buckinghamshire at Blickling Park, Norfolk by Joseph Bonomi (1794). Bonomi had worked in Adam's office and this design may be a source for his pyramid at Blickling, which was also surrounded by ruinous statues and urns, the stock-motifs of Neo-classical commemoration.[49]

The sarcophagus has a bas-relief of David Garrick and the project can be understood in the context of the eighteenth-century cult of genius.[50] Williams Wynn celebrated his hero Handel in the iconography of the house built by Adam at No. 20 St James's Square, and also played an important role in the Festival in Westminster Abbey in 1784. Eileen Harris [51] suggests that he had seen the design for a mausoleum to the musician in a wood in Staffordshire belonging to Samuel Hillier, and it is probable that Sir Watkin (who was spending lavishly on building projects) did intend this romantic vision to be built.

CW

49. See Roger Bowdler, 'The Mausoleum at Blickling' in *Apollo*, April 1998, pp. 11–14.

50. See Desmond Shawe-Taylor, *Genial Company: The Theme of genius in Eighteenth-Century British Portraiture*, (exhibition catalogue, Nottingham University Art Gallery and Scottish National Portrait Gallery), Nottingham 1987.

51. Eileen Harris, *The Genius of Robert Adam: His Interiors*, London 2001, p. 258.